ISBN 978-0-948545-30-6

published by
The New Century Press
11 Springwell Avenue
North End, Durham DH1 4LY
United Kingdom

printed and bound by
Prontaprint
85 New Elvet
Durham DH1 3AQ

Between the Woods and the Sea

The story of a cottage in Morvern

by

Christopher Bacon

with illustrations by

Celly Rowe & Heather Bacon

New Century Press
Durham 2010

This little book is dedicated to
Faith Raven
who has always supported us
and to the memory of
John

PREFACE

For nearly half a century I've been lucky enough to be the tenant of a cottage in one of the most remote and beautiful places in Britain: Inninmore, in Morvern, on the northern shore of the Sound of Mull. Throughout this time I've been going there as often as I could, usually several times a year, and in the earlier days for quite long periods, sometimes alone but usually with family and friends. Besides its remoteness and its beauty, Inninmore has all kinds of interesting features, including wonderfully rich wild life. There've been many changes over the years, and people have often told me that I ought to write about it all, so that the record isn't lost and the grandchildren can read about what their parents and grandparents used to do there. It's impossible to do justice to such a special place in words alone, but perhaps what I write will bring back memories for those who've been there and convey something of its special quality to those who haven't. My account is a very personal one, and other people, I'm sure, will see some things differently.

My tenancy has spanned two marriages, so the pattern of family names changes at different points in the story, as does the style of the pictures. For 20 years I used to go to Inninmore with my first wife, Celly; and latterly with my second wife, Heather. But whatever happened in our personal lives, we've all remained steadfast in our attachment to the place, and each has continued to visit, bringing new combinations of children, step-children and friends. I'm very grateful to both Celly and Heather for their help in writing this book and for their generosity in each contributing illustrations.

CONTENTS

Introduction   1

Chapter One: beginnings   3

    First sight   3

    Further developments   5

    Taking stock   7

    The path   10

    Clearing the path   15

    The grey boat   18

    Change of boat   21

    Repair work   25

    Furniture   28

    More repairs   31

Chapter Two: life at Inninmore   36

    Mod cons   36

    Visitors   39

    Unusual visitors   41

    Food and drink   46

    The fish trap   52

    Mackerel   54

    Beach harvest   57

Recreation   59

Sailing   63

Weather   68

Ships and aeroplanes   74

Fire   78

Medical problems   82

Chapter Three: the natural world   90

Eagles   90

Other birds   93

Flowers and plants   98

Trees   102

Small creatures   107

Rabbits   113

Larger animals   118

Chapter Four: the past   123

Geology   123

Archaeology and history   128

Shipwrecks   136

The last inhabitants   140

Envoi   146

Extracts from the visitors' book   148

Introduction

Once you've been there its enchantment will hold you in its spell forever. All I have to do to go back is just close my eyes. At once I'm standing on the beach with my back to the cottage, looking out across the Sound, where the mountains of Mull in various shades of green rise up in slanting folds, their tops disappearing into the grey cloud. Along the distant shore, except where it's obscured by the island, I can make out farm buildings and fields, and the occasional glint of a car as it runs along the coast road. To my right the waters of the Sound stretch westwards until they merge with the hills and the clouds. In stormy weather they bring rank after rank of steep waves to crash on the rocks that guard Inninmore Bay, but on calm evenings they lie tranquil and brilliant in the sunset. To my left, the view eastwards is limited by the island and by the promontories that project into the Sound, on the far side the massive headland supporting Duart Castle, on the near side the lowlier rocks that flank the entrance to Loch Linnhe. The children used to say the rocks to the east looked like the head of a crocodile, while the silhouette to the west, where the wooded shoulder of land runs down to the ruins of Old Ardtornish Castle and its stubby little lighthouse, was like the head of a rhinoceros.

I turn around to face the cottage. It sits just thirty yards from the high-tide mark in the middle of a half-moon bay. The bay is on the northern shore of the Sound of Mull, on the mainland of Morvern, but its remoteness makes it feel as if it's in the Hebrides. The cottage is small but well proportioned, with a roof of slate. It looks comfortable and welcoming, and blends with the surroundings as though it had pushed up through the grass like a grey-topped mushroom. Immediately behind the cottage a wooded V-shaped cleft splits the rising hills, dividing the craggy basalt cliffs on one side from the smoother contours of gneiss and granite on the other. To the north-west the escarpment that gives the place its name (Inninmore is the anglicisation of *aoineadh mor*, the Gaelic for "big cliff") rises abruptly to 800 feet, beyond which the ground goes up as far again more gradually to the summit of Glais Bheinn. The slopes below the cliff are covered right down to the shore with native woodland, through which runs the three-mile path from Inninbeg, the main route of access by land. To the north-east more

gently rounded hills extend over to Loch Linnhe. On this side the granite supports only a few stunted trees and shows through the coarse grass in bare patches of grey like a threadbare carpet. In front of the cottage is a natural lawn mown by sheep and deer, too bumpy for croquet but smooth enough to lie on comfortably and read a book. An irregular fringe of gorse, awash with yellow in the spring and still flowering even in mid-winter, separates the lawn from the beach. The shore has patches of sand, but is mainly pebbles punctuated by larger rocks, light and sculpted granite to the east, amorphous dark basalt to the west. A burn plunges down the cleft from the top of the hill, disappears into an alder wood where it splits into two, then emerges into the meadows, passes on either side of the cottage, and runs down to the sea by channels that change their course through the pebbles with every tide.

The cottage is stoutly built of gneiss and sandstone blocks, and has a generous eave at the front to give protection from the rain that lashes from the west. There's a central front door, a sash window on each side, one with four panes and the other with two, and a small skylight in the roof. All the woodwork outside is painted white. Inside, there's a small porch where coats are hung and boots deposited, leading on to a room on either side, to the left a sort of living room, to the right a sort of bedroom. There's another little room at the back, just big enough for a bunk bed and a ladder up to the attic. The floor, except for the bedroom, is of concrete, now worn smooth, and the living room walls have had the plaster stripped off to bare stone and mortar. There's a large open fireplace in the living room, raised a foot above the ground, with a large black kettle suspended over it. The bedroom has a smaller and neater fireplace. Apart from a Victorian brass bed the furniture is rudimentary, being made mainly of driftwood.

Chapter One: beginnings

First sight

I first went to Morvern nearly 50 years ago when my former tutor at university, John Raven, and his wife, Faith, invited me to spend a week with them at Ardtornish. The story goes that Faith's father, who was a director at Hay's Wharf in London (Faith likes to describe him as a wharfinger, which sounds like a posher sort of docker), came home one evening and said to his wife "By the way, Emmeline, I bought a place in Scotland from a man I had lunch with today." The place in Scotland was an estate of some 39,000 acres, mainly moorland, but including a huge mansion house, two ruined castles, a salmon river, a farmyard, three boathouses, numerous cottages complete with their inhabitants, and hundreds of cattle, sheep and deer. (Faith tells me this story isn't strictly true; but John would've liked it, so I've left it as it is.) The tradition at the big house was that guests should have a generous breakfast and then, if they wished, go walking, whatever the weather. On a wild September day I set off to climb Glais Bheinn, the hill that rises some 1,500 feet on the north side of the Sound of Mull. Well-wrapped and well-shod I headed up the path beside the river Rannoch, then turned right across a meadow and began the steady climb. It was hard going uphill through the rutted and tussocky grass, but eventually I made it to the top, and looking southwards could see the Sound of Mull stretched out way below, gleaming grey through the drizzle. I sat in the lea of a small cairn of stones and ate my sandwiches. A party of deer came into view about half a mile away. They were upwind and unaware of my intrusion into their wild territory. When I stood up to go they spotted me, stared briefly with necks stretched as if in disbelief, then trotted briskly away and out of sight. I made my way down into the wind to the edge of the escarpment. In places plumes of spray were being thrown vertically into the air as the water in the burns was blown back upwards by the force of the wind rushing up over the lip. These spouting burns, known as "The maids of Morvern," were said to have inspired Tennyson, who visited Ardtornish in 1853, to write "And the wild cataract leaps in glory." I leant into the gale, swaying my body to match the fluctuations in its strength. Suddenly a large brown shape swept past 50 feet below me and disappeared round the corner. It was an eagle, borne up by the surge of the wind. I'd been told there were eagles in Morvern, but this was the first time I'd seen one in the wild. I went further along the cliff to try and get another sight of it. As I rounded a corner, below me appeared the crescent of a bay, tucked into the hills and guarded on each flank by promontories of rock. The back of the bay was wooded, but the central part, divided by a burn, had obviously once been cultivated, though the two meadows now looked neglected apart from a few grazing sheep. Right in the middle, not far from the shore, was a little cottage with a slate roof. It too looked neglected: bushes grew up to the walls and the roof of a smaller building attached to it had fallen in. I sat wondering at the beauty and remoteness of it all, until the wind reached my bones and made me move on.

That evening at dinner I recounted what I'd seen. "That was Inninmore cottage," said Faith. "No one has lived there since before the war. It's become rather a ruin." "I'd love to repair it and go and stay there from time to time," I said, not expecting to be taken seriously. "Perhaps you should," replied Faith. "You'd have to ask my mother. She regards it as something of a nature reserve. She isn't keen on people staying there." Faith's mother, now a widow, was the aunt of a friend, so I'd always heard her referred to as Aunt Emmeline. She lived in the middle floor of the big house, and I'd met her the previous day as she walked along the road by the loch. After we'd exchanged greetings, she expressed her delight at the beauty of the place, as if she was seeing it freshly for the first time, although she must have walked that way on countless occasions since her husband had bought it on an impulse more than thirty years beforehand. Surely a person so appreciative of the natural world would want to preserve the solitude of Inninmore from the intrusions of a stranger? So there, for the moment, the matter rested.

Further developments

That visit to Ardtornish was also responsible for two other major themes in my life. At the time I first stayed there I was becoming disenchanted with my career in the British Council, which I'd joined on leaving university. Teaching English in Sukarno's Indonesia had been exotic and exciting, but sitting in the London office gave too much time to ponder what it was all about. I began to wonder if I could possibly make an entirely new start and become a medical student, but this seemed a pretty far-fetched fantasy, because, as a classicist, I'd done almost no science at school and I needed to go on earning my living. I shared my fantasy with John. I expected him to give me one of those understanding yet penetrating gazes and then to point out gently how unrealistic it was. Instead he at once phoned his brother-in-law, John Lipscomb, who was a consultant physician and happened to be staying in one of the holiday cottages on the estate (Garden Cottage, which later became the residence of the estate manager). That evening as the light began to fade I sat with John Lipscomb at a table by the cottage window that looks down the loch. He listened patiently while I laid out my fantasy. He looked at me intently as he asked me about my education, about my interests, about my aspirations. For what seemed an age he gazed down the loch. The lights of the sand mine at the mouth of the loch were reflected brightly in the water. Then he turned back to me. "I think you should do it," he said. "It won't be easy, but I think you should do it." He offered to put me in touch with a friend who was dean of a medical school. My spirits were up with the stars as I walked back through the darkness to the big house: those two hours of conversation in Garden Cottage might change the whole course of my life. Not long afterwards, having had an encouraging talk with the dean, I burnt my boats and resigned from my job at the British Council, and started on the 1st MB course at St Thomas' Hospital. At first doubts that I would ever get through and dismay at my dwindling savings made me wake at nights in a cold sweat. But after a few weeks I knew for certain that this new venture was right for me.

We were a motley collection on the 1st MB course, mostly people like me who were making a change to medicine from some other career: a linguist, a diplomat, a historian, a lawyer, two teachers, and various others. The historian was a girl called Celly Robertson. We struck up a conversation. I mentioned this very special place in Scotland, expecting her to be impressed. "Oh, you mean Ardtornish?" she responded, with irritating nonchalance. "I've been there too." By remarkable chance, not long beforehand Celly had stayed at one of the Ardtornish cottages in a reading party organised by another member of the Raven family.

Celly and I came to realise that we couldn't escape our entwined destinies and in due course we found ourselves married. The Ravens invited us to Ardtornish in celebration. We visited Inninmore together, and the idea of repairing the cottage came up once more. This time we were brave enough to approach Aunt Emmeline. She received us in her sitting room, which has one of the most beautiful views in the world, over the gardens as they slope down to the shore, along the wood-fringed waters of Loch Aline and across the Sound to Mull and its mountains fading into the distance. The view made you think that anything was possible in that room, and excitement vied with nervousness as we sat on the sofa responding to Aunt Emmeline's courteous but probing questions.

We hadn't planned a strategy, but for some reason, perhaps because she saw how we shared her delight in the natural world, after ten minutes' catechism Aunt Emmeline agreed that we might become tenants at Inninmore. There were to be certain conditions: we should respect the wild life, we must look after the cottage and preserve it in the old style, we must never use a gun and we should do our best to keep noisy strangers away. So began our association with this very special place, an association that has now lasted for 46 years, giving a constant seam of richness to our otherwise inconstant lives, a still point in our turning world.

Taking stock

It was agreed that for the first few years we should pay no rent while we carried out basic repairs, with the estate providing the materials. Since its abandonment nearly 30 years beforehand nothing had been done to maintain the building apart from occasional repairs to the main roof - without this vital measure the gales would have long since reduced the whole place to a ruin. Our initial survey of the work now required was daunting. The front door was off its hinges and the windows glassless and poorly patched with plywood, allowing wind and rain to sweep inside. The plaster in the living room was sodden and blistered off the walls, and such paint as remained was discoloured and peeling. In the western wall was a gaping hole, like the socket of a huge tooth, where a cooking range had been ripped out. There were bits of charred wood, several empty bottles and tins, cigarette packets and other rubbish. Once somebody leaves the first bit of litter, more somehow accumulates even though no one else comes. The only utensil was a very large black kettle without a lid, which hung over the fire from a hook behind the lintel. The floor was carpeted with sheep droppings, seasoned with soot washed down the chimney. The bedroom looked a bit better, though many of the floorboards were rotten and there was a smell of mice and mould. This room still had its small fireplace, but when we cleared away the pile of damp ashes and soot we found that the grate had rusted through. I went into the little room at the back and climbed on fish boxes to look in the attic. Again there were rotten boards and a smell of mould, and I was worried that the timbers might be terminally damaged by dry rot. There was a skylight looking out towards the sea, but it was small and the ends of the attic were too dark to see properly. The glass of the skylight was broken and there was a damp-edged hole in the boards beneath. There were numerous little piles of what looked like mouse droppings – or could it be bats?

At the eastern end of the cottage was the smaller building whose damaged roof I'd seen from the cliffs above. It had evidently been used as a byre, because there was a stall at one end and the floor was deep in litter, in which brambles, bracken and flags were growing in profusion. There was no door, and the three small windows had no glass. About two thirds of the back roof was missing, probably blown inside out by the force of the wind coming through the open door. The dense growth of brambles and the rottenness of the timbers suggested this had happened many years beforehand. Repairing the byre roof would clearly be a major undertaking, especially since all materials would have to be brought in by sea. But it looked like a very old building, simply but solidly built; it deserved to be preserved for its own sake, and it would make a useful workshop and storeroom.

Behind the north-west corner of the cottage was a small wooden shed with a roof of rusted corrugated iron that looked as though it had been a privy. A small burn ran past its door and down the west wall of the cottage. Water for drinking and washing was probably taken from another branch of the burn twenty yards to the east. Although its site in the centre of the bay had the attraction of symmetry, the cottage was badly sited for drainage, being right in the path of the main burn that came down from the cleft in the hills behind and tended to spill over during spates. We learnt later that this burn had once flowed in its entirety to the east of the cottage, but during a spate some years beforehand it had split in two so that part of it now flowed to the west.

During one of our early visits it rained heavily for three days, and we watched this western branch of the burn swell to ten times its normal size and force, until it began to dislodge stones from the base of the house wall. Something had to be done about it straight away. We decided to try and divert the course of the burn away from the building and through the bog further west. In the pouring rain we dug a new channel, sometimes using a spade and a

pickaxe, sometimes scrabbling with bare hands. We tried to dam up the existing course with the stones we were digging out, but at first the force of the water kept washing our fledgling dam away and the task seemed impossible. Then, after three hours of working without a pause, we saw the first trickle of water choosing to fork right instead of left, and following our new channel. Once this process had started, the water in the burn, hitherto our adversary, saw which way the battle was going and changed sides, allying itself with us to help deepen its new course. Gradually the old flow past the wall dwindled as we plugged the gaps in the dam and built it higher. At dusk we had to stop, exhausted but exhilarated, every inch of clothing soaked and wellies full of water. The next day the burn had scoured out a new course over a foot deep through the bog and down to the beach. After a week it was so deep and wide that we had to bridge it with a plank. We heaped earth on our new dam and planted grass and bushes to bind the rocks. The following year the house wall was dry, and a sandpiper set its seal of approval on the burn's new course by nesting under the plank bridge. Looking at the dam today it's hard to believe it was constructed by two pairs of hands in one wet afternoon: its base has become much more solid with many years' accumulation of debris, and alders and wild roses have grown over it to make it indistinguishable from the surrounding terrain.

The big barn

The path

The best land access to Inninmore is by the path that comes in from Inninbeg (a*oineadh beag,* "little cliff") to the west, traversing the slope about halfway up between the shore and the undulating crest of the escarpment above. Some people call it "the middle path," because it's also possible to walk along the edge of the escarpment, or at sea level along the shore. But the higher route involves scrambling down and up numerous little gulleys, and the lower route, passable only at low tide, involves scrambling over rocks slippery with seaweed, both exhausting journeys if you have a heavy pack. The middle path has probably been in use for centuries, though it must have taken ceaseless human effort to counter the constant assaults of the elements. Legend has it that before the war Dougie Cameron, who lived at the cottage, used to ride his motorbike along it every day to get to work. This is hard to believe today when you're working out how to cross one of the many little ravines that burns have gouged deep across its track. Although this story isn't strictly true (as we'll see later), there were once wooden bridges over all the burns, which made the path much easier to traverse. However in 1956 an exceptional period of prolonged heavy rain swelled the burns into mighty torrents that swept away all the bridges and gouged out ravines that have never been bridged again. The path is nearly three miles long, and the fastest you can do it, without a pack, is just under an hour. With a heavy pack or fractious children it can take twice as long, and with both at once it may take half a winter's day.

The rocky trot

On a fine day the beauty of the path lightens your load and shortens the distance. You start just below the steading at Old Ardtornish, at the elbow of the track that leads down to the bay. Here the rocks and sand are all of basalt, and its darker hue, together with the shade of the tall trees nearby, make this bay more gloomy (and in summer more midge-infested) than the open and part-granite beach at Inninmore. You set off across a stretch of bog, spangled with yellow flags in the spring, while a month later the surrounding slopes show a flush of bluebells beneath the green of the new bracken. The going is mainly firm but has treacherous patches in the winter. You have to locate the path correctly when you reach the bracken, otherwise you can flounder up and down the slope all day - some people have given up here and gone back home. After going half a mile through a pleasant hazel grove you come to the first and biggest of the burns, which you'll hear before you see. After heavy rain the torrent leaping down from the hills above gives you a wetting, or may even compel you to turn back. There used to be a large platform of rock in the middle that supported a two-stage bridge, but this was swept away in 1956 to leave a ravine about 60 feet wide. There's a rope stretched between the trees on either side to hold onto as your feet slip on the wet rock. This obstacle surmounted, you promenade beneath a stand of stately trees, mainly firs and beeches, planted some 200 years ago and now enjoying their last years of magnificence until one by one, shallow-rooted, they topple in the winter gales. Once you're out of earshot of the burn you hear the wind soughing in the pine needles high above, the string section of the orchestra, while the waves crashing on the rocks far below provide the brass.

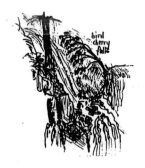

After a while the ground flattens out to an open stretch above a promontory of rocks jutting out into the Sound, called "Englishman's Point" (*Rubha an t-Sasannaich*). Who the Sassenach was and how he fared, I've never been able to discover, but in view of the past behaviour of my countrymen in this part of the world I suspect he may not have fared too well. Perhaps those that know are too polite to tell me. Here I should say that we've never sensed any resentment from the local people that an Englishman should come to tenant this very Scottish cottage; indeed the usual reaction is amusement that we should want to stay in a place so primitive and remote.

There's a large grass-covered rock beside the path here, a good spot to stop for a rest, swinging off your pack and letting the wind get to the sweat on your back. You'll usually hear the cronking of ravens from the cliff above as they see off buzzards and hooded crows that have intruded on their territory. Way below, you'll always see curlews poking about on the shore and one or two shags fishing off the rocks; and if you're patient and keen-eyed you may spot an otter foraging for shellfish among the kelp. When the sun's warm it's tempting to stay for hours, but in winter the wind soon nudges you on.

tick alley

As you progress eastwards along the path more of the Sound appears through the trees, and you catch glimpses of Duart Castle way down on the far side. Looking back to the west you'll see the silhouette of Old Ardtornish, and beyond it you'll probably be able to make out the car ferry plying between Lochaline and Fishnish, a toy boat trailing white threads behind it. In April the path here is redolent with primroses, and on a warm still day their scent can be almost overpowering. When the sweetness turns to a stench you know there must be a carcase nearby: the deer succumb to malnutrition and disease at the end of the winter, and come down from the hills and into the wood to die. Besides primroses in profusion, there are also violets, wood anemones, bluebells, celandine and many others. In the trees above, willow warblers and wood warblers, seldom seen but singing non-stop whenever the sun is out, provide the perfect musical accompaniment. In one stretch the path is bordered by massive rocks, fallen from the cliffs above perhaps centuries before and now covered with a deep padding of green moss. In the spring overarching hazels are festooned with the turquoise and yellow of lichen and catkins, and the dappled sunshine turns the scene into a fairies' grotto.

Inninmore Bay curves slightly inland so you don't see the cottage until you're about half a mile away. The first glimpse through the trees is always exciting and reassuring, like meeting a much-loved friend after a long absence. There's also slight apprehension. Have any strangers taken up residence? Is there a boat on the beach or smoke coming out of the chimney? Will the recent gales have done any damage? Even, God forbid, will the cottage have been vandalised? The path emerges from the wood, runs horizontally along a bracken-covered slope, then drops diagonally downwards to sea level. Picking up your pace now, you walk through an alder grove and across a bog, dodging the brambles and stinging nettles in what was once a drained and cultivated meadow. You cross the burn by a plank bridge, go round the corner of the cottage and you're at the front door. The door and the windows are closed, as you left them. There's total silence apart from the chattering of the burn and the cries of the gulls from the beach. Your old friend is unchanged and welcomes you back.

But on a wet day in late summer the bracken can make the journey miserable. It grows most strongly where there are no trees, leaning over the path from each side to join like Velcro in the middle, sometimes obscuring it so much that you struggle blindly and may lose the track. The bracken fronds brush the wetness into you from every direction, and although you start out hoping your clothes will keep you mostly dry, you soon have to resign yourself to a total soaking. Meanwhile brambles reach over with trailing hooks to snag you, and stinging nettles, lurking in ambush, seek out any unprotected skin. You can't get a firm footing on the wet and sloping earth, and your boots slip on the rocks in the burns to get repeatedly immersed, so that you soon feel water creeping down your socks towards your toes. Added to these discomforts is the awareness that with every step the ticks that lurk in the bracken are transferring themselves to your body. For a small child in a wet August the path has no delight.

The children made the path seem less formidable by breaking it into pieces and giving them names. First came Bishop's Bog, where my cousin Wynn Bishop once sank in up to his waist. Then Hazel Grove. Then the Big Burn. Then Rainbow Arch, where an oak trunk covered in moss, lichen and fungi leaned across the path. Then Picnic Rock. Then Blackthorn Tunnel, where the path seemed to go underground through a thicket. Then the Rocky Trot, where you had to pick your way through boulders that somehow found their way back every time you cleared them away. Then Robin Hood's Den, where a mass of ivy overhanging from the rock face gave you shelter from the rain. Then Bird Cherry Falls, a waterfall just above the path where a bird cherry used to grow. Then Primrose Dell. Then Tick Alley, an open stretch where the bracken grew thickest. Then Simon's Grove, a stand of spindly and unprepossessing alders made lovely by a visiting artist. And then, at last, the cottage.

Clearing the path

Robert Frost might equally well have written "Something there is that doesn't love a path." Or perhaps, although its charms are clear for all to see, the path doesn't love itself, and constantly tries to efface itself by reverting back to wilderness. Boulders of all sizes roll down the slope and come to rest on it, the first flat piece of ground they encounter. We've never witnessed big rock falls, but we see evidence of their passage in the fresh scars where they've been detached from the cliffs and in the line of smashed trees that marks their headlong career down the hill. The children ask what to do if they hear an avalanche coming. Blithely we tell them "Lie down and the rocks will bounce right over you," but the reality doesn't bear thinking about. After prolonged rain mini-landslides slip down and obliterate complete sections of the path. Where the slope is steep and it's hard to keep your footing, the path tends to slip downhill in a series of little loops that diverge further and further from the original course. The many burns that cross the path seem intent on its erosion: the winter rains convert the dried or trickling beds of summer into torrents that gouge out ever deeper and wider incisions.

The vegetable world conspires with the forces of nature in this campaign of obliteration. The soil is thin and the trees are shallow-rooted. As they grow bigger they're uprooted by the winter storms, or in summer the added windage of their foliage makes them vulnerable to lesser gales. Two or three trees fall across the path most years. Some are so massive that it takes some time to clear them away, and meanwhile you have to climb over a trunk or clamber through horizontal branches, your pack snagging annoyingly. Brambles are a perennial pest, every season sending out a fresh set of sharp-hooked branches to trail over the path and catch on clothes and rasp across exposed skin. They're not so bad for adults, who can press them down them under a boot, but for small children they rear up waist-high in horrid menace. And in time brambles can even make the path more crooked as people and sheep take diversions to avoid them. In high summer the open stretches of the path are obliterated by bracken. Although it grows only six feet high, its extensive network of rhizomes makes it the largest plant in Britain, and it's almost impossible to eradicate...

Most winters I try to enlist a posse of navvies to stay at the cottage for a few days to work on the path. Each is required to bring a stout pair of boots and a bottle of whisky, and in return for his labours is given a staple diet of porridge for breakfast, cheese sandwiches and apples for lunch, and sausages for supper. At first it was men only, but after much lobbying partners were invited too, and the cuisine became more varied. Every day after breakfast we set out in a line with saws, choppers, picks and spades, singing "Hi ho, hi ho," to toil all day at our dwarf-style engineering. Regrettably the Snow Whites refuse to stay at home and do the house-work but insist on coming with us. Cutting through a fallen tree trunk with a cross-cut saw is tedious, and if you don't judge the right place to cut the saw will get trapped; so in recent years we've abandoned our Luddite purity and taken a chain-saw.

The brambles are best tackled with stout gauntlets and long-handled loppers, but satisfaction at cutting your tormentors down to size is spoilt by the thought that you'll have to do it all again next year. The bracken you can't do much about, except, as you walk along the path in the spring, keep adjusting your step so that your boots snap off the emerging shoots while they're still fragile and hooped, like the embryos of some alien life forms.

You can usually move even the biggest boulder off the path if two of you sit side by side with backs against the slope pushing with four legs. At first the boulder doesn't want to budge. You keep pushing and start to grunt. Still no movement. You grunt a bit more and wonder if the boulder has a root like a wisdom tooth, but you don't want to be the first to suggest giving up. Then at last it stirs slightly in its bed. Sensing victory, you push even harder. Abruptly it decides to get up, hesitates for a moment at the edge of its socket, then goes bounding away down the hill until it crashes onto the rocks by the shore. We try to make the deeper burns less difficult to cross by placing rocks in strategic positions, and sometimes by securing guide ropes to the trees on either bank. But the biggest engineering task is restoring the path to its original track where it's become deflected downwards. First we have to decide which of the many affected stretches is most in need of restoration, and how long a segment we can tackle in the time available. We map out the line of the original track, which may be some ten feet higher up the hill, and start working at it from each end. We cut into the many years' accumulation of earth and rocks with pickaxes and spades, uprooting any bushes and trees that have grown there. Whenever possible these are preserved for re-planting elsewhere: in my garden in Yorkshire there are two oaks, several hazels and hollies, and numerous primroses that first saw life on the path to Inninmore. We have to cut quite deep to make the new track broad and strong enough to walk on, and it may require buttressing with boulders and branches. The buttress is then planted with shrubs and grass, like the sides of a motorway, to bind the earth in the winter rain. We root out any brambles growing just above the new stretch, otherwise they'll force people to walk below it again and quickly undo all our efforts. It's hard physical work, but in those surroundings, with the camaraderie and the delicious smells of earth and leaves, the fun of it outweighs the aches, the scratches and the blisters. When it begins to get dark, or earlier if it's raining hard, we go back to the cottage. We have a restorative swig of whisky, stoke up the fire and light the candles, argue about whose turn it is to cook, wash in the burn, eat our sausages, drink some more whisky and go early to bed. When the whisky runs out we go back home. As we walk back along the path, we get the satisfaction of noting that what was the worst stretch of path when we arrived has now become the best.

The grey boat

Among the early problems was how to transport loads of heavy timber and slates from the estate to the cottage. The path was out of the question, and the estate's launch, an old lifeboat, chosen because of Aunt Emmeline's mistrust of the sea, didn't have much space for cargo. One day, nosing round the many outbuildings in the estate yard, we came across an old clinker-built open working boat. It was about 16 feet long and very solidly built, but the grey paint was peeling and there were gaps between some of the bottom planks. It hadn't been used for years, and at some stage, perhaps at the beginning of the war, had been brought up from the loch to be stored under cover. Johnny Graham, an estate worker then in his eighties, said it was an old boat when he was a boy. It had been used, he said, amongst other things, for transporting bulky materials to Inninmore and Eignaig, the cottage four miles further on, round the corner up Loch Linnhe. What more fitting than to re-commission it and resume the voyages it had made so many years before? Here I should acknowledge our dependence on the good will and practical help of the estate manager and his assistants. Looking back, I can't think why they were so patient with us and how we took it all for granted. The manager at that time, Alastair MacAndrew, was immensely helpful, and we wouldn't have got anywhere without him. It wasn't always to be that way, and when Alastair moved on a few years later we learnt how hard it could be, without good will, to get things done in the Highlands. We caulked the bottom boards with bitumen and repainted the boat in warship grey. Nobody could remember her original name so she was known just as "The grey boat." Now that she was being cared for again, she turned back into a lady and changed from "it" to "she." Alastair arranged for her to be taken down to the loch for her first launch for over thirty years. At first she leaked so much that she quickly sank onto the sandy bottom, but as her boards took up the inflow diminished until it became manageable by frequent bailing. She could just be propelled with her two long oars, but it was hard work and certainly wouldn't do for the five-mile journey down Lochaline and along the Sound. Alastair kindly let us borrow an old Seagull outboard motor, whose two horse-power was just enough to propel the heavy boat and whose simple construction matched my limited mechanical skills. The noise of someone trying to start a recalcitrant Seagull will be forever imprinted on our memories.

Our first cargo was timber for the roof, plus two bags of cement perched on top to keep them dry, and a selection of tinned food, mainly baked beans and pilchards. We had to leave a clear space to allow constant bailing, but despite this the tins quickly lost their labels in the bilge water. It was a calm day, and although our load weighed us down, no water came over the side to add to that coming through the boards. Loch Aline is sheltered by hills except

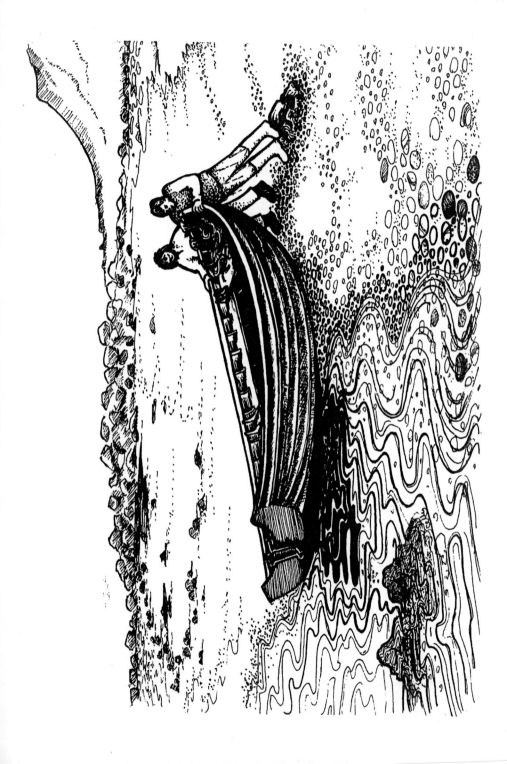

in a southerly gale, but the swirling currents at the narrow entrance can buffet a small boat about when the tide is running fast. Once out in the Sound you turn eastwards, keeping well out if the tide's with you, closer in if it's against. If you know the water well you can take advantage of the eddies. When close inshore you make a note of what's been washed up on the beach for a later visit to collect firewood. The tide runs fast round Ardtornish Point (it flows in from east to west in the Sound), and when wind and tide are opposed the sea there can get unpleasantly choppy, with steep little waves coming at you from unexpected directions. After that, apart from another choppy patch off Englishman's Point, it's a steady haul down to Inninmore Bay. Our first trip by boat was straightforward. Apart from one short stop for refuelling, the engine went without a splutter, and we congratulated ourselves on the ease of the journey as compared with the labour of carrying a load along the path.

A later journey, made with my friend Mike, who was in the navy, was very different. Emboldened by our previous success, we put on a much heavier load, so that the freeboard, about 18 inches with the boat empty, was reduced by half. The loch was sheltered from the wind by the hills to the west, but little cumulus clouds were moving briskly through the sky. Mike assured me it was no more than force three and we set off down the loch. The first hint of trouble was the corrugated appearance of the sea ahead as we passed through the mouth of the loch. As we went out into the Sound we realised the corrugations were ranks of steep waves running before the wind. I took fright and wanted to turn back, but as a timid ex-airman I couldn't argue with an experienced sailor relishing a challenge. Soon it was too late for turning back and we had no option but to go on with the wind behind us. The waves coming up astern looked as though they must break over us, but each in turn lifted us high, surged past hissing and threatening from either side, then dumped us down again. If we tried to turn across the sea we would undoubtedly be swamped. If the engine cut out, dowsed by water or having run out of fuel, we'd wallow across the waves and founder. The oars were partly obstructed by our load and we wouldn't be able to hold the bows into the wind. Mike sat aft minding the engine, keeping us strictly stern to the seas, shouting "Like a bird, like a bird" as each wave hoisted him high. I sat forward on the timber and thought we would soon be more like the fish. The fuel tank usually only lasted for two thirds of the journey, and would be almost impossible to refill in the wind and tossing boat. It looked a long way to swim to the shore, especially without life jackets, and there were no potential rescuers in sight. We could hang on to the timber, but we wouldn't last long in the cold sea of early summer. The boat was driven fast by the following wind, but it still seemed an age before at last we reached the lea of the promontory that shelters Inninmore Bay. The fuel ran out just as we approached the shore. We poled the boat into the shallows, wobbled ashore with trembling legs and collapsed on the beach.

Carrying heavy things up the rocky beach was exhausting, and we learnt to leave the load on board and edge the boat up towards the high tide mark as the tide came in. At first we had no mooring, and since the boat was too heavy to drag up and down, we used to beach her at high tide and wait till another high tide before taking her out again. Once, on the morning that we had planned to go home, we woke half an hour late and just missed the high tide. We rushed straight down to the beach in pyjamas and struggled to pull the boat down the two feet required to float her, but the tide receded faster than we could move her and we had no option but to accept a 24-hour delay in departure.

Change of boat

The grey boat was a dependable but stubborn friend for many years. Once afloat she was solid and seaworthy, and she carried heavy burdens without complaint, but getting her in and out of the water nearly broke our backs. She spent the winter under cover in a shed at Ardtornish, and at the end of our last visit of the season we had to manoeuvre her in the shallow water onto to her trolley and haul her a little way up the shingle, to be towed away later by a tractor. This was a cold and laborious task, and usually had to be done at first light to allow us time to complete our long journey home. In the early days, after seeing to the grey boat, we used to walk the five miles to Lochaline to catch the ferry, then hitch-hike from Oban back to London, seldom arriving before midnight.

One September, while visiting the big house, we met the estate's boatman, who very kindly agreed to help us get the grey boat out of the water when we left two days later. He was an old-time Norfolk fisherman called Lester Green, who couldn't quite bring himself to retire and came to Ardtornish each summer to skipper the estate launch. He liked to wear waders, and this encouraged us to think that he would do the coldest part of the job, which was to stand in the sea and manoeuvre the boat onto its trolley. As we approached the shore in the early mist, there was Lester, standing on the jetty, impressive in sou'wester, oilskin and waders. We edged the boat up to the shingle and waited. Lester didn't move. Reluctantly I lowered myself into the water, and once again felt my legs go numb with cold as the wetness crept up to my midriff. Once I'd got the boat positioned on the trolley Lester came and helped us haul it out. "I'd hoped," I ventured, "that you might've been able to wade in and help us get the boat on the trolley, with such a good pair of waders." Lester was unabashed. "They leak," he said. He told us that the next week he was returning to Norfolk to prepare for the winter's fishing. We asked him what fish he would be catching this winter. He stared into the distance with that far away look of the deep-sea mariner. We imagined fierce storms, icy rigging and great hauls of cod. Then he turned to us and said "This winter it'll mainly be cockles." At his age he was entitled to come in from the cold, and I only make fun of him because he used to make fun of himself.

Much as we came to love the grey boat, our aching backs eventually drove us to conclude that we needed something easier to handle. As soon as we were earning again, having at last qualified as junior doctors, we set about acquiring a more modern boat of our own, sharing the cost with Richard and Karilyn Collins, who'd been fellow students at St Thomas's. Richard went to the Boat Show in London and picked out the Orkney Longliner, a sixteen-foot working boat made of fibreglass to a traditional design. She was very similar in shape to the grey boat but not nearly so heavy. She had a small area of decking in the bows and a collapsible cuddy to provide shelter for passengers, though the helmsman had to stay exposed as usual in the stern. We never got round to giving her a name of her own, and by analogy with her predecessor she's always been just "the white boat." She spends most of her time lying in the boathouse at Inninbeg, a handsome building under the trees constructed some 150 years ago for the smaller craft of Old Ardtornish House. The spring tides wash up into it, but at other times the boat has to be hauled down and back up a steepish slope of rocks on a trolley, so that we try to time our arrivals, and more importantly our departures, to coincide with high water. Once the boat is launched we row her through the breach in the fish trap, which forms a miniature harbour, and onto the sandy beach to load up. The curve of the bay where the boathouse is situated faces south-east, and when there's a brisk south-easterly the forceful slapping of the waves may make it impossible to launch or re-house the boat.

To make life with the boat easier at Inninmore we put down a mooring, in the shelter of the rocky promontory on the west side of the bay. At high water the boat rides sixty yards out, but at the lowest tides it's stranded on the sand beside the fish trap. The mooring was made mainly from local materials. We took a large wooden box that had been washed up by the tide, balanced it on the wheelbarrow, and filled it with concrete mixed with sand and pebbles from the beach. In the concrete we immersed an iron bar bent into a circle, with a small loop protruding from the surface. When the concrete had set, we wheeled the barrow down to the edge of the water at low tide, tipped the box off and partly buried it. We shackled a chain to the loop and attached a buoy, one of the many delivered by the tide, to the other end. Despite its amateur construction this arrangement worked well, except that about every four years the chain became thin with rusting and had to be replaced. As you look out of the cottage window you see the boat riding easily at her mooring in the shelter of the rocks. This is always a comforting sight at the end of the day, and seems to add to the homely spirit of the place. At first we had no little boat to serve as a tender, so, except at low tide, someone had to wade or swim out to get the white boat in. In time we acquired a very small dinghy, which gave a lot of fun to the children as well as being a tender – until it was stolen and we had to get wet again until we could afford another.

We found that the upper end of the mooring chain rusted much faster than the lower end, presumably because there's more oxygen in the water nearer the surface. To make the chain last longer we used to remove it and store it in the byre in the winter. This meant that on the first visit the following year we had to find the block, which had been half buried in the sand and might now be camouflaged by seaweed. The search can be fun on a warm day at low water, but soon loses its appeal when you have to wade around with the bottom half of your body paralysed with cold and the top half assailed by midges. To speed up the process I took a careful note of cross-bearings from features in the surrounding landscape and recorded them in the back of the visitors' book. This worked well until a non-mariner tore out the page and used it to light the fire.

Meanwhile the grey boat had made her last voyage. She had been left out on her trolley at the side of Loch Aline just above the beach, where cattle from the nearby meadows sometimes go to browse the seaweed. An inquisitive bullock thought the boat was a good target for butting practice and made a hole in her hull. It was decided that she wasn't worth repairing, and she was taken up a little way into the meadow and turned over. The familiar round shape of her hull could be seen there for many years, rushes and flowers growing through the hole and crowding round her sides, her keel a look-out post for pipits and sandpipers. Then one spring we saw she'd disappeared completely. It seems that she'd been broken up for firewood by a stranger, a sad fate for a boat that had given stalwart service for over 150 years.

Repair work

All the rafters and boards on the back of the byre roof were either missing or rotten, but many of those on the front were sound. An experienced builder would no doubt have taken the whole lot down and started again from scratch, but I wanted to preserve what I could of the old craftsmanship, and somehow it seemed less daunting to do the job piecemeal. So I set about putting in new rafters one at a time, setting the base into a wall plate, and bolting the top either to the existing front rafter if it was sound, or to a new rafter laid alongside it. This was slow work, and since we could only be there for part of the medical school holidays, it took three years to complete. The slowness at least allowed time for the swallows and pied wagtails that used to nest in the ruins to find alternative accommodation. The wagtails simply moved to an ivy-covered cliff at the end of the beach but the swallows disappeared completely. We sadly missed their swooping flight up and down the bay and their twittering as they came to feed their young. After a few years, still missing them but without much hope of success, I fastened a little platform of wood under the eave of the main cottage in case they happened to return prospecting for a new site to nest. On my next visit, as I rounded the corner of the cottage on arrival, a swallow flew out and I could see the heads of chicks sticking up inquisitively from a mud cup stuck to my platform. Aunt Emmeline would have been pleased.

Many of the slates that had fallen off the roof had been broken or washed down the beach by the burn in spate. We got replacements from an abandoned cottage near the estate yard, carrying them laboriously down to the loch and loading them onto the grey boat. There's still a pile of surplus and broken slates in the

grass behind the byre, now serving as an apartment block for a colony of slow worms.

We cleared an accumulation of muck out of the byre and came across a neatly cobbled floor underneath. There was an old manger on the wall at one end, and when we had pulled it away we found the outline of a fireplace. It seemed that this small building had once been a dwelling for humans, but was converted to a cattle byre when the present larger cottage was built alongside. It had thick walls, and when made secure with a new roof, a door and glass in its three windows, it felt like a little fortress against the elements. With surplus rafters we constructed a really solid workbench, to which we fitted a large vice. On this bench, which takes up much of the room, over the years various handymen have done all sorts of repairs, and craftsmen of all ages have fashioned numerous masterpieces, including wooden spoons and bowls, two handsome stools, a Noah's ark, various classes of sailing boat, a chess set and an assortment of building bricks for babies. Perhaps my own best effort was with an ancient and stubby piece of plank I'd found among the rocks. Its shape and the handhold cut into it suggested it had once formed part of the transom of a rowing boat. Years of exposure to salt and sun had produced a silver patina on its surface and abrasion by pebbles had rounded its edges, but its weight showed that the wood within was still sound. As I planed and sanded it down, the beautiful grain of well-seasoned pitch pine emerged. I cut it into two pieces and shaped them into chopping boards for the kitchen. I gave one to a friend but took the other home, where it's still in use 25 years later. As we chop the parsley we imagine how long ago in its previous existence the board used to ply up and down the Sound – and perhaps once supported the back of a loquacious poet when Tennyson was rowed over from Oban. However my other attempts at carpentry haven't had quite the same success, but have too often reflected the pattern of my life: it's only when the job's nearly finished that I see how I should have started it.

Getting glass for the windows was more difficult than you might expect. We carefully measured the frames and gave the dimensions to the estate handyman, who kindly cut the panes for us. At that stage we had no car, so the journey back from the estate yard involved carrying the glass in a pack for eight miles, the first five along the track that skirts Loch Aline and turns left along the Sound, the last three, down to Inninmore, over the hazards of the middle path. We congratulated ourselves on arriving with the glass intact and brewed the kettle for tea. We'd already cleaned the debris from the frames, so all we had to do before fitting the glass was line them with putty. We carefully lifted up the first pane and applied it to the gap. It was the wrong size. Perhaps we'd got the wrong piece. We tried another, but that wouldn't fit either. Nor would the next. Four of six panes were out by more than an inch. In time annoyance gave way to amusement that the West Highland inch must be different. Not wanting to embarrass the handyman, who'd been very friendly and helpful, we decided to get replacement glass from Oban, which we'd wanted to visit in any case. This required a more complicated journey. We had to get up early and walk all the way round Loch Aline to the village, twelve miles in all, to catch the ferry to Oban. Prolonged exertion without breakfast is always exhausting, but the boat trip down the Sound made it all seem worthwhile. We waved to the cottage as we went by, ruefully reflecting that by sea we'd covered in 15 minutes the same distance that had taken us nearly four hours' hard walking. The ferry took a wide sweep towards the shore of Mull and called in at Craignure, which would later become our main source of supplies. Then on down the Sound, with Duart Castle massive on the right and Lismore lighthouse elegant on the left. We docked at Oban and found a hardware shop that sold glass. We handed over the measurements, triple-checked, and were assured the glass would be ready to pick up before the ferry sailed back in the afternoon. We sat on a wall by the quay eating fish and chips and admiring the fishing boats, then went to explore the town and buy provisions and tools. Our glass was ready in good time for us to board the ferry and sail back to Lochaline. Silent with tiredness, we trudged the 12 miles back to the cottage, my pack stretched with the glass, packed meticulously in bunches of newspaper, Celly's laden with the rest of the shopping. It was dark when we arrived and we got straight into our sleeping bags without even lighting the fire. We were aching and exhausted, but consoled by the thought that next day the windows would be properly glazed and at last we'd be rid of the plywood patches.

But that's not quite how it turned out. We could scarcely believe it when next morning we found that one pane was again wrongly cut, and the plywood had to go back in. If this was a way of settling old scores against the English, it couldn't have been more painful and effective. We had to wait till the following year before we finally succeeded in getting a pane of the right size safely delivered and installed. At last we could sit at the table and gaze out unobstructed. Since then we've been especially conscious of the value of glass, and one of the first things we always do on arrival is to clean the windows so that the clarity of the view isn't spoiled by dried spray. Visiting footballers, however, have not always shown the same respect, and there've been a few breakages. Fortunately in recent years we've been able to get replacement panes quickly and easily by motoring over the Sound to Craignure, whose facilities now include a builders' merchant with a metric tape measure.

Furniture

When I first looked into the cottage the only furniture was a wobbly bench in the form of a plank resting on fish boxes. We've continued the tradition of making furniture from driftwood, different visitors contributing different items as their skills and the materials available allowed. In the early days, before cargoes were packed in containers and fish boxes became plastic, driftwood was more plentiful. Today you seldom find a good balk of timber or a sturdy wooden box, though there are numerous tangles of nylon rope and assorted plastic containers. We extended our beachcombing by prospecting from the boat for several miles along the shore, picking up wood of all shapes and sizes, either for construction or for firewood. Shores facing the prevailing wind were the most productive, in particular the rocky stretch to the west of Ardtornish Point, and the inlet just before the promontory that flanks the entrance to Loch Linnhe. The wind that brings the jetsam also brings choppy seas, so we could only go in close when it was calm and the boat wouldn't bump on the rocks. If we found a piece, such as a tree trunk, too large to lift into the boat, we simply hauled it into the water and towed it slowly back. Good pieces of wood were stacked in the byre to dry; some bits have been there for years now, awaiting the creative inspiration of a carpenter.

As well as bits of wood the sea has delivered lots of other useful items to our beach, including a ladder, a log basket, a good pair of sunglasses, two clothes' baskets, a wooden mallet, plastic buckets, lots of fish net (from some of which we made a hammock), a deck chair, buoys of various sizes and colours, many trainers and wellington boots (not usually in pairs), a boathook, a brand new football, several oars (also annoyingly unpaired) and a straw hat. Everything that floats will eventually come to those that wait on the lea shore of an ocean. Once we picked up a navigator's chair, with tall legs and a blue leather seat, which was drifting in the tide far out in the Sound. It was a day of total calm, when you could see a fish jump a mile away. As the tide came in after breakfast we saw what seemed to be a stick poking obliquely up out the water. It drifted back the other way at teatime, and our curiosity made us row out to see what it was. The chair was in perfect condition, and had no doubt been thrown overboard, together with its occupant, by a skipper enraged at being given the wrong course. It remained in the cottage for many years before being promoted to a smarter residence elsewhere.

The only other piece of conventional furniture was a Victorian brass bedstead. This was a wedding present from Faith, and came from a bedroom in the big house that was being refurnished. It's a simple bed that had no doubt seen much service, but its arrival at Inninmore was dramatic and somewhat surreal. Faith had kept her gift a secret, and the first we knew of it was when we looked out of the front window one misty morning to see two men in waders coming out of the sea and up the beach carrying a double bed. They had brought it round on the old lifeboat, with Faith also on board to witness our surprise. After a mug of tea and some predictable jokes they waded back out to their boat and departed, leaving us to try out our new item of furniture in private.

The first piece of furniture we made was a table to go by the window in the living room. Its top is a large wooden pallet and its base a framework of heavy timber, so it feels comfortingly solid. After 40 years of use its surface is polished smooth except where candles have been allowed to burn too low. It has sampled spills from a thousands meals, been splashed with paraffin from the lamps and with all sorts of drinks, witnessed hundreds of card games from underneath, seen the covers of countless paperbacks, and worn holes in the elbows of many jumpers as their wearers sit and gaze out of the window. The benches beside the table are made from hatch

covers, with a recessed handle at each end, set on stumps of pine trunk. At the back of the room there's a dresser; its back is made out of an old door thrown up on the beach, with shelves attached to the upper half and a cupboard lower down. There is a worktable, made from another door, against the side wall. In the middle of the room there are two easy chairs, their wooden frames dove-tailed by the most skilful of many visiting carpenters and upholstered with fish netting. From the ceiling above the fire hangs an essential piece of equipment, a home-made drying rack that can be moved up and down by a system of rope and pulleys. It has four bars each eight feet long, and on a wet evening becomes a multi-coloured wall of steaming cloth.

For the bedroom, to accompany the brass bed, we made a chest of drawers out of four fish boxes. It's big enough to hold a basic holiday wardrobe for two, but if you leave clothes there when you depart, the mice will quickly take up residence. Each drawer still displays its mark of origin: *Macrae, Duthie and Walker, Aberdeen*; *Caley Fisheries* (twice); and *Lochinver Fish Selling Co Ltd, no unauthorised use* (a prohibition ignored by the mice). The bedroom also has a table, much less substantial than in the living room but useful for reading in seclusion. When the children learnt to crawl the bedroom furniture was augmented by a playpen, which was made from a large baker's tray as base and wooden slats as sides. When the children got too big for the pen we turned it upside down and used it as a bedside table, until the woodworm took hold and converted it to its fourth and final vocation as kindling.

The little back room has a two-tiered bunk bed, made of a timber frame and sleeping surfaces of solid mahogany. These too look like huge baker's trays but were in fact salvaged from a wreck. Over the centuries many ships have foundered in and around Inninmore Bay, and this will be the subject of a later chapter. The most recent was the *Ballista*, which was blown on to the rocks at the western end of the island in 1973. Her owners salvaged what they could then left her to the sea. She lay there for about a year, her tilted hull partly exposed at low tide and just her funnel showing at high water, until eventually she broke up in the winter gales and disappeared. During that first year I rowed out for a closer look. It was a calm day, and at low tide I climbed in through the forward hatch to see if there was still anything worth taking. I explored gingerly, my shoes slipping on the sloping surfaces, which were now slimy with weed. At the back of the forward cabin were some bunk beds, with their sleeping trays still in position. They were just what we wanted. I managed to manoeuvre two of them out through the hatch before the rising water stopped me. I planned to come back for more later, but for the next few days the wind was too strong, and by the time we visited again the wreck was totally submerged.

More repairs

After a century of assault by woodworm the attic floor was friable and powdery, and all of it had to be replaced with new boards, well soaked with Rentokil. The little skylight at the front didn't let in much light, so we put two additional skylights, made on the spot to our own design, in the back slope of the roof. The force and angles of the rain soon found out their flaws, and leaks have been a recurrent problem. In the absence of scaffolding we get up onto the roof outside by a system of ropes and ladders. We throw a rope, its end weighted with a stick, right over the roof, and haul up our little step ladder, straightened out, so that it lies snugly on the pitch. We anchor it by tying the end of the rope to a wheelbarrow full of stones, and climb up to it with the piece of ladder we found on the beach. The apex of the roof gives you a wonderful view of the mountains and the sea, but makes you a more conspicuous and less mobile target for midges. Once the attic was safe and better lit, it could be used as an overflow dormitory, with space for four lilos, and as a storeroom, while still keeping its traditional role as sanctuary for mice, bats and bluebottles.

The wooden floor in the bedroom downstairs was so rotten that the legs of the bed sank into it. When we took up the boards we found the joists were rotten and wet, and water was trickling over the bare earth beneath them. We dug a trench outside the back wall to improve the drainage, renewed all the joists, and replaced the old floor boards with chip-board (the estate was now having to be more economical) – one short sentence to write, but many hours of work plus two well-laden sea journeys to achieve.

Testing the relationship

Meanwhile we'd been steadily stripping the loose plaster from the walls of the main room. Much of it was damp and came off easily, but the more adherent patches had to be chiselled off. The stone underneath was irregular and rough, but we decided against re-plastering. The gaping hole that served as a fireplace smoked terribly and was unusable in certain wind directions; sometimes the wind seemed to be deflected by the cliffs so that it blew vertically down the chimney. By trial and error we found we could reduce the smoke to tolerable levels by decreasing the vertical dimension of the aperture, which we achieved by raising its base and by hanging a heavy timber beneath the lintel. We built up ledges on each side that would keep food warm and dry out firewood or wet boots, and we placed a metal grill between the ledges so that pots could sit immediately over the flames. When we scraped away the soot on the large kettle that was there when we arrived, it proved to be a very fine piece made of copper, though sadly it had lost its lid. This kettle is usually suspended from a chain attached inside the chimney so that warm water is readily available, while a smaller and much inferior kettle sits on the grill for making tea.

The fire consumes a lot of wood and most of the heat goes up the chimney. Firewood is an important part of life at Inninmore. Everyone is encouraged to do ten minutes' collecting or cutting every day, and on departure it's a point of honour to leave a good supply for the next visitor. It's a dismal start to a visit to arrive on a wet evening and find no logs, either in the basket by the fireplace or in the former privy behind the cottage that serves as a woodshed.

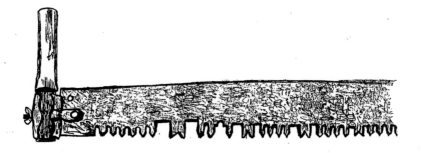

Seasoned driftwood provides the best burning, but when wet it first has to be dried out on the ledge of the fire. The woods along the lower slopes of the hill have plenty of fallen branches, but by the end of the summer you have to go further afield as supplies nearby are used up. Occasionally a whole tree falls and keeps you supplied for a year. Ash is much the best for general use, though gorse stems, despite their thinness, yield more intense heat. Cutting living trees has always been strictly forbidden, apart from an attempt at coppicing the alder grove at the back of the bay, soon discontinued because alder is too slow to dry and then too quick to burn. A saw-horse, made of surplus roof timbers, and a chopping block stand outside the west wall of the cottage. A bow saw is best for everyday cutting, and visitors are routinely advised to pack a new blade with their toothbrush. For tree trunks and other larger pieces there's an old-fashioned double-handed crosscut saw. Using it is a severe test of a couple's compatibility, sweetly satisfying when you're in harmony but quite infuriating when you're not - rather like rowing as a coxless pair. With regard to individual skills in wood-cutting, I never cease to be amazed by otherwise intelligent people who pick up an axe and try to chop wood across the grain.

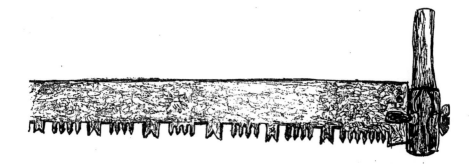

The small and rather ugly fireplace in the bedroom had been intended for coal, but when fuelled with wood didn't burn for long or give out much heat. At an early stage we therefore installed a Jotul wood-burning stove, our most expensive purchase ever (apart from the white boat), which we carried round by sea. The Jotul was a handsome shade of green and heated the room well, but the rain coming down the chimney and long periods without use caused it to rust through after a few winters. More recently we've fashioned another open fire, which incorporates the original cast-iron surround but has a new inner arch inlaid with pebbles from the beach and ledges on either side for candles at bedtime.

After a few years of repairs there was a change of estate manager and work at the cottage became more difficult. Alastair, under whose benign eye the estate had been happy but unprofitable, was replaced by Ranald Coyne, who was charged with the task of tightening things up. Under the new regime it was no longer possible to borrow equipment or to order materials through the estate, but everything had to be obtained through our own efforts. This usually involved a special trip to Oban, which required a ferry journey and took up all the day. We weren't able to go on using the estate's outboard motor, so we dipped into our savings and bought a second-hand one for ourselves, which was fine, except for the bother of transporting it from and back to home at each visit. We learnt to steer clear of the estate office as much as we could, because our transactions there, no matter how politely intended, always seemed to end in unpleasantness. Looking back, I can see now that we'd been spoilt by previous generosity, and that from Ranald's more business-like perspective we must just have been a nuisance.

Other staff on the estate were unfailingly friendly and helpful, and never seemed too busy for an encouraging chat. I can't write about them all, but I must briefly mention Chubby Ives, who'd been working on the estate as a shepherd since before the war. He was a large man, enormously strong, who in his prime had been the shot put champion at the Morvern games. He seemed to know everything there was to know about the estate, past and present, and his Highland brogue gave an authenticity to his tales. He lived at Ferry House, near the mouth of Loch Aline, with his wife Maggie, whose father was shepherd before him. He looked after the sheep on the eastern half of the estate, so Inninmore was in his parish and we saw him often. He kept up a keen interest in sport. One Saturday morning we encountered him way up on the hill striding out purposefully. He stopped to greet us but for once didn't linger for a chat, so we knew something must be wrong - perhaps he was in a hurry to rescue a sheep in distress. He looked anxiously at his watch and turned to go, exclaiming "I must away now or I'll be late for Grandstand." Besides his duties as a shepherd, for nearly 40 years Chubby looked after the lighthouse at Old Ardtornish Point. In the early days he used to have to keep special receptacles filled with carbide and water, which, when mixed, generated acetylene to light the lamp. In the 1960s gas cylinders were introduced, while today the light is powered by solar panels, with batteries as back-up. Chubby now lives in retirement at the opposite corner of Loch Aline, in a cottage beneath the old castle of Kinlochaline. Arthritis prevents his getting about but he's never short of company for long. During the morning I spent with him recently there were repeated knocks on the door and half a dozen people looked in for a chat. Chubby no longer does the shot put but he still watches Grandstand (or its present-day equivalent). And he keeps a treasure chest of memories.

Chapter Two: life at Inninmore

Mod cons

This chapter could be brief. There are no mod cons at Inninmore.

But perhaps it's worth describing how we manage without them. The burn 20 yards to the east of the front door provides an unfailing supply of fresh water. The burn has its origins in the rain and snow that fall on a huge tract of moorland above, and the water is purified and aerated as it cascades from the cliff edge down a series of waterfalls to the bay It's cold even in late summer and always tastes delicious – or rather it doesn't taste at all. If ever a deer has fallen in and died upstream we haven't noticed. We collect the water in a small churn, holding about two gallons, which we keep by the door of the main room. When the burn is low you may have to make a little hollow to sink the churn deep enough, and during a spate the water is slightly tinged with peat. If you have to go and collect all your water you notice how much you use: for four people the churn needs filling about ten times a day. It makes you think what it must be like for a family enduring a drought in Africa.

We wash either in the cold water of the burn, or in a bowl of water heated in the big kettle. Even in mid-winter you can wash all over in reasonable comfort, standing in front of the fire. Small children – and some small adults – may prefer to sit in the tin bath. Even mature flesh looks attractive by the firelight, as Rembrandt showed so well. If you feel the need to immerse yourself completely, which fortunately I never do, you can lie down in the burn, stand in the waterfall half a mile away or run down into the sea. For young ladies of a certain age the daily hair wash is an essential routine. They cavort by the burn like naiads (but respectably clad in T-shirts and jeans), trailing their tresses and shrieking as the icy water penetrates to the scalp. To a mere mortal like me the sudden tingling is excruciating, poised midway between ecstasy and masochism, and a hair wash once a week is quite enough. Teeth are cleaned over the burn. If you don't aim carefully, gobbets of saliva frothed with tooth paste miss the water and fall on the protruding rocks, so that you can tell when it last rained by the density of the white splodges.

the tin bath

The midges determine how thoroughly the dishes are washed. Washing up is done in a bowl on a pile of fish boxes outside the front door. When there are no midges it's quite a pleasant experience, with beautiful views all around and the sound of the sea and the gulls. But if the midges are out they'll quickly drive you frantic, as you rush to get the job done while scrabbling with soapy hands to keep the growing cloud of tiny assailants at bay. Often the dishes have to stay dirty till the wind comes up.

Now comes the bit people are most curious about. How do we manage without a toilet? There are plenty of bushes nearby so peeing is not a problem, though it calls for a waterproof and wellies when it's wet. Ladies can't afford to dawdle when it's midgy, while in a gale gentlemen must remember to stand with backs to the wind, like daffodils in March. For more serious matters there's a choice between heading for the bracken with a spade, or, when the tide's coming in, going down to the rocks on the shore. I know of no other place where you may see an eagle or an otter as you go about your daily routine, and I always take my binoculars. In fine weather, rather than just being a chore, going to the loo can be one of the high points of the day. We've resisted advice to install proper facilities, partly because the terrain won't allow a septic tank and chemical toilets are so repulsive, but mainly because the lack of a toilet is a very effective deterrent of the faint-hearted and the over-civilised.

Mains electricity was brought to Inninbeg about 15 years ago, but it'll never make economic sense to bring it on to Inninmore – unless one day someone finds a seam of uranium (strontium was discovered at Strontian, not far away) or starts a fish farm (see page 130). Meanwhile we go back a century and light ourselves with oil lamps and candles - though for the first few evenings after arrival your hand automatically reaches out for a switch as you go into a room. The absence of electric lighting makes you appreciate the darkness. I think it was Thoreau who observed that electricity destroys darkness whereas oil lamps illuminate it. However, after trying all sorts of lamps we've come back to using simple candles. Basic paraffin lamps don't give much more light than a candle; if you turn them too high the glass blacks over, and if you turn them too low the wick disappears into its burrow and won't come out again. Pressure lamps, like thoroughbreds, can be highly-strung and temperamental, and they spoil the silence with their hiss. Good old-fashioned candles don't leak paraffin in your pack, are understood by everyone, give out their light silently and make a pleasing smell when extinguished. You need three to read a book, or five if the print is small. If you look up from your book and try to gaze out of the window, all you can see is the reflection of five candles with the wraith of your face behind them, like an icon in a shrine. Some visitors like to use empty bottles for candlesticks, but the accumulation of wax looks grotesque and we prefer to mount our candles on pieces of slate.

When it comes to the disposal of rubbish, we're ever mindful of Aunt Emmeline's wish that we should keep the place unspoiled. Anything that will burn, from scraps of food to fragments of plastic, goes on the fire, which is a form of recycling in that it keeps us warm and helps to cook the next meal. Empty bottles, jars and tins are put in a bin to await ritual burial at sea. We take the bin half a mile out in the Sound, fill the empty containers with water one by one and drop them to sink into the depths. We like to think the tins will make good homes for hermit crabs before rusting away, while the glass will be ground by the action of tides and gales until it's converted to the pretty multi-coloured pieces of sea glass that end up on our beach. When we haven't got the boat we carry the bin at low tide to the end of the rocky promontory that flanks the bay. You have to make sure that each item is sufficiently full of water to sink, and if one stays afloat it's bombarded with stones until it goes down like a bombed warship. Quite often, when we've not been able to dispose of all our rubbish properly before we leave, we carry it in bags back with us in the boat or in our packs. Our two main complaints when strangers have stayed at the cottage are that they haven't left any firewood or that they haven't cleared up their rubbish.

Visitors

We leave the front door unlocked so that anyone can go in when we're not there. Ranald, who had a thing about security, ordered us to get a padlock for the door and grills for the windows, but somehow we never got round to it. The cottage has always served as a shelter and resting place for travellers, whether they come by sea or by land, and we like to keep up the tradition. In the summer yachts often moor in the bay, which is marked on the charts as an anchorage, while dinghies and canoes land on the beach, all in increasing numbers in recent years. Walkers are less frequent, and consist mainly of people out for the day while staying elsewhere on the estate, though there are occasional serious long-distance hikers with heavy packs. To all of these we're pleased to be able to offer a temporary sanctuary where they can sit down and rest under a dry roof, and perhaps light a fire to get warm and make a cup of tea. Mugs and teabags are put out ready. We don't mind people staying overnight, so long as they observe the rules, but we're not so keen on those who take up residence for days, use up all the firewood and leave the place littered with their rubbish. Most people who visit uninvited are considerate, but some regard the unlocked door as a license to stay as long as they like and to treat the place as they wish. If we arrive to find unexpected occupants, usually they leave gracefully, but a few argue that the cottage is a bothy and they got there first, so it's not them but us who should leave. Once or twice, when my talk of repairs and rent and council tax has fallen on deaf ears, I've had to drop a gentle hint about the law. Since mobiles came on the scene it's been possible in theory to contact the police, but the nearest policeman is in Strontian, 35 miles away by a narrow winding road and then by the path. The worst aspect of these encounters is not the mess people leave but the feeling that the place has been defiled. We've never seriously considered locking the front door, because well-behaved travellers would be deprived of shelter while the badly-behaved would simply break in. We've suffered remarkably few thefts in 45 years, mainly because there's little that's worth the effort of carrying away. The worst losses have been to do with boats: an old winch, not used for many years but still serviceable, was removed from the beach, and a small fibreglass dinghy was taken from the byre. We keep tools, utensils and spare food up in the attic, and for a few years we made the mistake of closing it off with a trapdoor and padlock. Some visitors seemed to regard this as an indication of stored treasure within and repeatedly broke in, only to find nothing worth taking. We've now reverted to leaving everything open, though I may try and hide a few particularly vital items, such as a pair of binoculars or an unfinished bottle of whisky.

From the outset we've left a visitors' book on the table in the main room. The front page starts with a welcome, names the landowner and the tenants, and very politely sets out the basic rules: please keep the place tidy, replace the firewood, respect the wildlife, don't build a bonfire on the front lawn, and resist the temptation to take up permanent residence. Seven volumes of visitors' books, in the form of hard-backed notebooks, have now been filled. The first volume was installed and inscribed in 1972 by John Raven, who encouraged us in the early days and liked visiting to botanise, especially in the bog, where he found species not recorded elsewhere in Morvern. It's impossible to do justice to John's remarkable personality in a few lines here, but for anyone who knew him his rare and benign spirit will always be a part of the enchantment of Ardtornish.

Most visitors come by sea, some having sailed a long way from home, and there are entries in the book in French, German, Dutch, Italian, Spanish and (I think) Finnish as well as English and Gaelic. Predictably, certain themes keep recurring: "What a beautiful place," "The weather is lovely," "It's very wet," "Thank you for leaving the door open," "The midges are terrible," "We've seen four seals," "We like the furniture," " I caught five mackerel," "You ought to get a toilet," "We think we saw an eagle," "We found a dead deer," "We definitely saw an eagle," "I'd like to stay for ever." The entries of yachtsmen tend to be more laconic, as in a ship's log, for example "Yacht "Pandora" ex Oban moored Inninmore Bay 1340 hours 3/7/85 en route Tobermory." At the other extreme some entries, perhaps written after a good supper and a few drinks, run to several pages. Some authors use the visitors' book like a journal, each day recording the weather and all their doings. Some wax lyrical and some may even be moved to verse. Some show off their erudition with literary allusions or pastiche. Some are charmingly zany and some are downright scurrilous. A few are really quite witty. Several have suggested recipes, both real and fanciful, for cooking on an open fire. The children have always enjoyed making their contributions, sometimes illustrated, and the seven volumes present a record of how their priorities and sense of humour, as well as their handwriting and spelling, have changed as they've grown older. When we arrive at the cottage after a period of absence, the first rituals are to walk down the beach, come back and light the fire, then read the new entries in the book. It's given me a lot of satisfaction, as I've re-read them all in the course of compiling this reminiscence, to reflect how many people over the years have enjoyed visiting Inninmore and staying in the cottage for a while, and how our decision to leave the door open has been so richly vindicated. One entry in the visitors' book is of very special interest: it was made in July 2000 by a lady called Margaret McAllister, who came by boat (she didn't say where from) to see the place where her great great uncle and aunt had reared a family of nine children a century and a half beforehand.

To give you a flavour of the visitors' books, selected extracts (but only a tiny fraction of the whole) are appended at the end of the main text of this narrative.

Unusual visitors

Over the years hundreds of people have visited Inninmore while we've been there, and no doubt many hundreds more when we've not. A few individuals stand out as being unusual. The most remarkable of these came during a very hot spell of weather in August. It had been airless and sticky the previous evening, and we'd lain awake for many hours listening to the gulls before finally getting to sleep. We woke late and had breakfast sitting outside in our nightclothes, still half asleep and heavy-limbed. A heat haze was already shimmering over the beach, and even the gulls were now silent. Then, looking to the west, about half a mile away we saw a solitary dark figure that wobbled like a mirage in the haze. The figure gradually became more substantial, and turned into a man walking along the shore towards us. He came steadily closer, and as he emerged through the gorse bushes we saw a person of wiry build and unkempt beard, with a wide-brimmed hat on his head and a pack on his back. He strode straight up and stood before us, took off his hat and flung it to the ground, and stared at us with intense and glittering eyes. "I'm looking for that traitor, Judas Iscariot," he announced. There was a pause while he held us in his gaze and we digested his request. "I'm sorry, we haven't seen Judas Iscariot this morning," I eventually replied. "Would you like some coffee?" We didn't know whether to be amused at what might be a practical joke or scared at an imminent attack by a maniac. One always feels more vulnerable in pyjamas. I grasped my breakfast knife behind my back, and we were relieved when he accepted the offer of coffee. Celly went to make it and the man sat down on the bench beside me. There was the pungent smell of a man who had walked many miles in the sun. He addressed us earnestly as he sipped his coffee. "The Lord is sending down punishments because we haven't caught the traitor," he confided. "Have ye noticed the heat?" We agreed that it had been unusually hot. "Have ye noticed the midges?" Yes, we had noticed the midges. The conversation continued on these lines until lunchtime, when he agreed to share our bread and cheese, and then to go with us in the boat back to Inninbeg. We motored down and landed him on the beach. He took off his hat, waved us goodbye and walked away up the track. We later learnt that he was well-known around the west coast as a religious vagrant who went from place to place preaching and getting food and shelter as best he could. Despite the violence of his language he had never hurt anybody or stolen anything, and he seemed to be entirely benign. We were rather disappointed that he didn't visit us again.

Another unusual encounter, with a visitor with a different social background but the same flair for a striking opening remark, came a year or two later. I heard the crack of a rifle from the direction of the sea, and looked out to see a large inflatable boat

with three occupants passing close to the island. Through the binoculars I could make out two young men wearing deerstalker hats and holding rifles, and an older man sitting in the stern. The boat changed direction towards our beach, and I went down to see who they were and what they'd been shooting at. As soon as the boat touched the shingle the older man, stocky and red-faced, stepped ashore and marched towards me. When still about 20 yards away, "I'm blunt," he proclaimed, and held out his hand towards me. His manner seemed to confirm his self-appraisal. "Delighted to hear it," I murmured, at a loss for the appropriate answer. "Major Hubert Blount," he repeated affably, "just come round from Eignaig, but usually live in Norfolk." Relieved that he didn't seem to have heard my first response, I told him my name, saying that I too usually lived in Norfolk. "One of the Norfolk Bacons, eh? How's my friend Edmund?" Sir Edmund Bacon was Lord Lieutenant of Norfolk at the time. I had to confess that, so far as I knew, we weren't related. "What are you doing at Inninmore then, Bacon?" His tone had changed to that of a superior officer addressing a subaltern. I explained how Mrs Hugh Smith had very kindly allowed us the tenancy of the cottage. "And how's my friend Emmeline?" he asked. The major evidently moved in distinguished circles. He told me that he was the tenant of Eignaig, the cottage three miles away up Loch Linnhe, even more remote than Inninmore. He'd taken it, he said, mainly for the stalking that went with the lease. The two young men in the boat had been practising for the forthcoming season by taking pot shots at cormorants sitting on the rocks. A comment about shags and stags came to mind, but it didn't seem quite the moment. Like our earlier visitor, Major Blount didn't visit us again.

Skip, however, stayed for quite some time. We found Skip and his dog in residence when we arrived at the cottage in February for our first visit of the year. He told us he'd been there since the autumn, when he had set out in an old Firefly sailing dinghy from Oban, not knowing where fate would take him. There was a gale blowing and he lost his rucksack overboard, but knowing this must be decreed, he didn't try to retrieve it. The wind drove him past Lismore lighthouse and out into the Sound, until eventually he ran ashore on the shingle beach at Inninmore. Nearby he found an empty cottage in a beautiful setting, and he knew this must be where he was destined to stay. Somehow he managed to survive through the winter. He told us that he hadn't touched our food supplies and hadn't even looked inside the attic. The large pile of shells in the bushes showed that mussels, winkles and cockles must have been his staple diet. We heard later that he had once or twice been seen walking to the village to pick up his dole money and buy basic provisions. He greeted us in friendly fashion, but he wouldn't entertain the suggestion that he might move elsewhere the next day. He had to stay at the cottage, he said, until fate told him to go elsewhere. But he agreed to move out of the bedroom for the duration of the visit and to sleep on a pile of fish netting in the byre. His dog had evidently shared the bed with him and we spent some uncomfortable nights scratching until we got some flea powder.

Skip himself was a gentle young man in his mid-twenties, long-haired and unshaven. He was clearly intelligent, and had had a conventional upbringing and education, but his spirituality had then driven him to reject the conventional world. He was something of a mystic and a hermit, his other-worldliness enhanced by starvation and smoking pot. He kept an illustrated diary, full of curiously distorted observations, philosophical comments, exhortations to love and to peace, runic symbols and strange prophesies. He had a reverence for the natural world and seemed very much in harmony with the spirit of the place, so we were happy for him to stay on at the cottage for longer. We didn't think Aunt Emmeline would have disapproved. He used minimal resources, and explained how he got warmed five times by a single piece of wood: going to find it, cutting it down, bringing it back, cutting it up and finally burning it. He spent a lot of his time making little boxes from deer bones. He would cut a section about three inches long from the hollow shaft of the femur, slice off the top to make a lid and fashion end-pieces from slate. The whole thing was meticulously worked and polished, and when finished looked like ivory. We had hoped he would leave us one to remember him by, but we think he sold them all to help pay for his pot. The last time we saw him communication was more difficult because he'd taken a vow of silence for peace. When we went back in May he'd gone, leaving a larger pile of shells, a new generation of fleas and a rune denoting "Home" branded into the beam above the fire. His sailing boat lay crippled on the beach for several years, until it was so broken by the gales that we used it for firewood, except for the spars and stays, which we've been keeping in the byre until we can think of a new use for them.

The most unusual visitor of them all was so improbable that for a long time I didn't believe he was real. One morning, when the children were still quite young and up to all sorts of tricks, they ran into the cottage to tell me there was a bear in a boat not far from the shore. "It's enormous," they said; "eight feet tall at least." "Don't be silly," I replied. "There aren't any bears in Scotland. And if there was one it wouldn't be that big and it wouldn't be in a boat." They insisted that I should come and look, so to humour them, when I'd got to the end of the chapter I put down my book and walked down the beach. There was no boat to be seen. I expected them to laugh and say "April fool" (even though it was mid-July). They persisted with their story, however, and I began to wonder whether, with their minds full of animal stories, they might in fact have seen something vaguely bear-shaped - such as a roll of fish-net hung up to dry - that they'd misidentified. I only found out they'd seen exactly what they said they'd seen many years later, when I learnt that a showman wrestler, Andy Robin, and his wife Maggie, sometimes used to come past Inninmore in a boat with their tame grizzly bear.

MAGGIE. GRIZZLY AND ROBIN
HERCULES. BIG SOFTY
WERE. HERE
2." JULY 1981.
Thank you.
THE SHERIFMUIRE INN
DUNBLANE 823 285.

They'd acquired the bear as a cub in 1975 and reared him lovingly to be a gentle giant 8 foot 4 inches tall and weighing half a ton. They called him "Hercules." In time Hercules became an international star: he featured in numerous advertisements, wrestled with James Bond in the film *Octopussy*, appeared on Hollywood chat shows, played in cabaret at Las Vegas, promoted the Miss World competition, caddied for Bob Hope at Gleneagles, and received greetings from the Queen and from Ronald Reagan. On one occasion in 1980, while filming on Benbecula, he went off on his own for over three weeks, and had to be shot with a tranquillising dart before being carried back to the mainland in a net slung beneath a helicopter.

Hercules didn't come ashore when the children saw him that time. But he did on another occasion, and he may even have gone into the cottage - perhaps to try out the bed and the porridge. An entry in the visitors' book dated 2nd July 1981 reads:

Maggie Grizzly Andy Robin & Hercules Big Softy Were Here

Beside the inscription is a simple drawing of a sitting bear. When I first read this entry, and for many years afterwards, I thought it was a joke, or perhaps referred to a teddy bear brought by a child to meet our resident bear "Inninmore Ted." But I now know that it recorded a visit by the most famous of all the people who've ever been to Inninmore.

Food and drink

At Inninmore your appetite is stimulated by fresh air and physical activity, and you soon get so hungry that there are seldom any left-overs. There's a lag of a few days before the new appetite kicks in fully, and before it fades again, so for the first few days after you go back home you go on feeling the need for a cooked breakfast. We always start the day with porridge, and if we remember it's been put in the saucepan to soak overnight. The first person up lights the fire. If it's not your turn it's good to linger in bed on a wet morning and listen to the crackle of the kindling while the rain drums on the roof. We use enamelled metal plates and bowls, so as not to add to the collection of broken china on the beach. We always have a cooked breakfast, usually bacon and eggs, or sometimes mackerel or sea trout if we've had a good catch. If there aren't enough eggs to go round we make eggy bread: you cut the requisite number of slices of bread, soak them in the beaten eggs and fry them. The frying pan sits on the metal grid that straddles the fire, its ends resting on the ledges at either side (the fireplace was constructed to fit the dimensions of the grid). There are two kettles, a small one sitting on the grid to heat water quickly for tea and coffee, and the big one hanging on the chain above for the washing up. We make toast on a toasting fork held over the embers when the fire's beginning to die down.

The saucepans and frying pan hang on hooks along the shelf that runs quite high up on the back wall of the kitchen. The row of round black circles of various sizes is an image that comes immediately to mind when you think of the room. We don't bother to keep the outsides and bottoms of the pans clean because they're constantly exposed to the fire, and if you try to wash them you simply make everything else in the bowl go black. Underneath the shelf hang mugs of china or enamel, and then various cooking implements like tin-openers and ladles. Basic foods such as jam and rice live in a little cupboard on the wall, while perishable foods like vegetables and meat go in an aerated but fly-proof container that hangs in the byre. When we go to Craignure we buy fresh milk at the store. We keep it partly submerged in the burn to stop it going sour so quickly; this is also the best method for cooling white wine. When we can't get to the store we mix powdered milk, which can be surprisingly like the real thing, so long as you get rid of all the lumps: we once got everybody to taste samples of pasteurised milk and powdered without knowing which was which, and some of us couldn't tell the difference.

In the summer we let the fire go out after breakfast, though we may briefly revive the flames to make mid-morning coffee. It's surprisingly easy to bring a small kettle to the boil with a few carefully placed sticks and judicious puffs from the bellows, which hang beside the hearth. Many people puff the bellows too strongly and blow a black hole in the embers. The secret is to choose a spot where the wood's just smouldering and blow it steadily but gently, without disturbing the embers, until the flames are established. One of the most infuriating misdeeds of visitors is to hold the bellows too close to the fire so that it burns a hole in the leather. Good bellows are hard to find, and I was delighted when an obstetrician colleague, skilled at stitching in awkward places, brilliantly repaired our present pair with a piece of leather from an old boot. In the early days we sometimes used Primus stoves, which are quick and easy but noisy and smelly and much less homely than a wood fire. Lunch is usually cold, except in the winter when we have soup. We always take a loaf or two of bread in with us, but once that's run out we bake our own. We mix the dough on the chopping board that was once the transom of a boat, and put it in a basin on the fire ledge to rise. We acquired an old tin oven from the abandoned kitchen at the big house. This baked our bread for several years but then fell apart; whereupon an engineering friend made a replacement, complete with sliding door, from industrial steel. This fits neatly on top of the grid over the fire and looks as though it will last for ever. Baking requires steady heat for about an hour, so a good supply of dry wood, preferably gorse, is essential, plus frequent gentle puffs from the bellows. The smell of the baking bread is as delicious as its taste. Surprisingly, the last housewife of Inninmore, Emma Cameron (see page 144), missed out there and didn't make her own bread, though perhaps she didn't have such a good oven. She did make scones, however, which we too make, on a large griddle bought from an antique shop. On the griddle we also make pizzas, which hadn't reached the Highlands in Emma's day.

Our evening meal is more leisurely. In the summer we often have fish, in the winter it's usually stew, wonderfully comforting after a day's hard work in the wet. For the first two days after we've arrived, or after a trip to the stores, we may have sausages or chops. *Haute cuisine* is wasted at Inninmore because everything tastes equally delicious. Vegetables present a problem: fresh ones are heavy to carry in, while the dried variety tend to be insipid. When we were visiting the estate we often looked in on what was once the kitchen garden to the big house, where Mr and Mrs Lamb used to grow and sell vegetables and all sorts of other plants. You could be sure that anything you bought was fresh out of the ground. The kitchen garden and its cottage, in their quiet ways, have been a source of many blessings over the years: crisp cabbages, luscious raspberries, shrubs for our garden in Yorkshire and, a long

kitchen at Inivermore

time ago, a new direction in my life. We've tried growing our own vegetables at Inninmore, as the Camerons once did (see page 143), but if you're not there all the time it's hard to prevail against deer and weeds. We cleared a small patch behind the cottage, cutting away brambles and bracken and removing piles of stones, some so big they had to be levered out with a crowbar. We fertilised it with barrow-loads of bladder wrack and kelp from the beach, and protected it with a wire fence six feet high. The first year we grew some wonderful potatoes, unblemished in the virgin soil, and carrots untouched by the fly. But the roots we've grown more recently have acquired the usual pests and diseases, and visitors aren't always interested in keeping the plot weeded. Sometimes the crop isn't harvested and next summer we dig out a nasty mess of old tubers, brown, sprouting and ravaged by slugs and rot. We tried eating stinging nettles, and soon discovered that only young shoots are edible and have to be gathered in large quantity because, like spinach, they boil down to almost nothing. We also tried various types of seaweed, which all turned out to be pretty unpalatable. But then a party of French canoeists landed on the beach. With shrieks of Gallic glee they identified a succulent variety, quickly gathered a bowlful, washed it in the burn, tossed it in olive oil and garlic, cooked it briskly over a petite travelling stove and made it taste delicious. The only other plant we've eaten is sorrel, which makes a bitter but agreeable component of salad.

In July we get a bowlful of small gooseberries from the two half-wild bushes that grow by the ruin behind the cottage, the only produce left by earlier inhabitants. In September the brambles turn from curse to boon by giving us copious blackberries. If you have the patience to pick a basketful of hips, stew them and strain the pink sludge that ensues, you can make delicious jelly from the wild rose. There are also plenty of sloes, but we never have the gin needed to do them justice. The most dainty and tasty fruits are the wild strawberries, which ripen along the path and around the cottage in early summer - though it takes ten minutes to pick a decent mouthful. Bilberries grow here and there on the slopes, but the deer keep them too closely trimmed to produce fruit in any quantity. The children's favourite dessert, "Spaceman's Delight," doesn't yet feature in Delia Smith, so I'll include a brief recipe here.

Take as many bananas as there are children. Peel but don't slice. Slit each banana lengthways down the middle, and insert three pieces of milk chocolate in the slit. Wrap the bananas individually in a double layer of foil and place on the grill over a glowing but not smoking fire for 10 minutes. Allow to cool before serving.

After dinner, while the adults sip their coffee and their whisky, the children toast marshmallows, impaled on a long fork, over the fire. There's a fine art to this. Toast them too little and they're rather boring, toast them too much and they burst into flames. But just right they're delicious.

By far the best natural source of protein is the sea, whose bounty is detailed below. We've eaten rabbit only once, in the unusual circumstances recounted later. In the early years rabbits were still plentiful at Old Ardtornish and on the island. I tried to teach myself how to use a bow and arrow accurately enough to shoot them, but I couldn't even hit a fish box at 20 paces and had to give up. We tried catching them with snares, but we lacked the skills of Emma Cameron (see page 144) and had no success. It's tantalising to see so much fresh meat wandering around in the form of red deer, but, mindful of Aunt Emmeline, we've never seriously thought of trying to kill one. We have however nurtured the ridiculous hope that one day we might see a deer or a sheep fall over the cliff and break its neck, but all we've ever found is stinking corpses many weeks old.

When all else fails there's always the store of tins in the attic. For over 40 years successions of kind visitors have left surplus tins. Understandably they eat the nicer things they've brought and leave only the more boring, and there are many vintages of pilchard, corned beef and spam. In time the labels go brown and peel off, and you can't be quite sure what you're opening; without the label the better brands of dog meat look and smell much the same as some brands of tinned stew. Also in the attic are numerous packets of dried soup and vegetables, which look attractive in the shop and are easy to carry, but have somehow lost their appeal by the time you're choosing what to have for supper. When we haven't got the boat we sometimes resort to dried potato, which tastes nothing like potato and looks like Polyfilla but makes a change from rice and pasta.

Most people drink more water than usual when they're at Inninmore because it tastes so pure and cool. Cleverly marketed it could sell in bottles by the million. To my amazement, one visitor, worried about the quality of the water at the cottage, laboriously carried in several plastic bottles full of water from another Scottish source to keep her pure and uncontaminated during her stay. We have frequent brew-ups of tea and coffee, the latter usually powdered, though a few devotees insist on bringing beans and a grinder. Teabags, like soup packets, have a natural tendency to accumulate and you may find a venerable vintage. Evenings are often made more convivial by a bottle of wine, which is about the only luxury that's given space in the pack. But the drink I most associate with Inninmore is whisky. Spirits and liqueurs always taste best in their country of origin because they've undergone centuries of adaptation to the local environment. Whisky is no exception. It goes perfectly with the mists, mountains and physical discomforts of the Highlands. It has great medicinal powers. It relieves aching bones and stiffening limbs. It restores the flagging brain and stimulates the wit. It's the only sure remedy for midges (see page 110). It reduces flatulence and aids digestion. The antiseptic properties of the alcohol, traditionally used to preserve laboratory specimens against centuries of decay, protect against infection in the mouth, throat and stomach. I'm told that, if whisky is applied to the soles of the feet, it hardens the skin and prevents blisters, but I've never been able to spare any for this purpose. It plays an important part in male bonding, making the drinker feel more congenial and, in the candlelight, look more congenial, than he did earlier in the day. In a group whisky should be drunk straight from the bottle, not poured into glasses, which merely increases evaporative loss, risks spillage and adds to the washing-up. Passing the bottle round fosters mutual trust, each drinker relying on the man before him not to take more than his share and not to leave any spittle. And when the bottle's empty all can agree that it must be time to go to bed.

The fish trap

The fish trap is of a pattern found at several places along the west coast of Scotland, and there's a similar one in the bay next door at Inninbeg. These traps were built in the 18th century when the local population was much larger, but most were put out of action by being breached in the middle after the Game Fishing Act of 1870 made it illegal to catch salmon and trout by fixed engines. The trap at Inninmore escaped deliberate destruction, though it's been half obliterated by natural erosion. Ranald ordered us to breach it in case an excise man saw it and held him responsible, but somehow we never found the time. The trap is sited in the curve of the western end of the bay. It consists of a semi-circle of stones, about 80 yards in diameter, with the sump towards the sea and its two wings coming up the beach, so that its long open diameter is parallel to and 20 yards below the tide mark. It was originally about four feet high throughout its curving length, but over the years waves and silt have reduced its height by half. We tried building up the walls again with stone, but the task proved to be beyond us, the bigger boulders being too heavy and the barnacles shredding our hands. So when we want to make the trap operational we have to restore its original height with chicken wire fastened to wooden stakes driven into the sand at its landward base. We brought in two coils of wire from Oban, hiding them under timber in the byre in case Ranald should find them and deduce what they were for. It takes nearly three hours to drive in the stakes and to lay out and tie the wire, so it's only worth doing when you think tide and weather are propitious.

The trap is intended mainly for sea trout, and works only on dark nights when the tide's very high. The fish come close into shore attracted by the fresh water of the burns, and as the tide recedes they don't see in time that they're being encircled by the emerging walls of the trap. As the water gets shallower they get driven down into the sump, until eventually they're stranded on the sand. It's a sad end for magnificent creatures that have just crossed the Atlantic, but it must have been a life-saving addition to the diet of the ill-nourished humans who first built the trap.

In our early days sea trout were plentiful throughout the summer months at Inninmore, and little ones could often be seen leaping out

Fish in the Trap

of the water as they swam just off the shore. They added a very welcome addition to our diet, and provided great excitement to those prepared to get up at 2 am, because the moon in its perversity ensures that the highest night tides always reach mid-ebb in the early hours. Dark windy nights are the most productive, the fish then being less aware of the encircling walls of the trap. You somehow wake yourself up - unless you've managed to stay awake reading – pull on a thick jumper, trousers, an oilskin and wellies, and set off down the beach with a torch. If it's a clear night the brilliance of the stars will force you to pause and gaze up for a while, re-charging your soul with wonder and reminding yourself of your littleness. There'll usually be a satellite making its slow and steady track across the heavens, while a shooting star means there must be fish. On a stormy night you hurry on down to the water, hugging your clothes to you and wondering whether it's all worth it. Sometimes you'll be too soon: the water in the sump of the trap will still be too deep and you'll have to return to the cottage, revive the fire and make a cup of tea. You go back 40 minutes later, wondering whether to tempt providence by taking an empty bucket. The first signs that there's something in the trap are ripples coming from the top of the netting as the fish knock into it, and little bow-waves surging back and forth. Then the water gets low enough for you to wade in and look down with your torch. This is the moment of truth. On many nights, especially if the weather's calm, all you'll see is crabs scuttling over the bottom and perhaps a shoal of darting sand eels. You trudge back up the beach, wondering why you ever left the warmth of your bed. But on a good night there'll be dark shapes, sometimes more than a foot long, dashing from side to side as they try to evade the beam of your torch, like aircraft caught in a searchlight. They're so strong and agile that it's hard to catch them until the water's almost all drained away. Then you have to decide whether they're big enough to keep, or whether you should throw them gently over the wire to swim away. Once or twice, in the early days, there were so many large fish, weighing around five pounds or more, that we had to throw most of them back, because the flesh of sea trout is so rich you can't eat it for more than two successive meals and we haven't got a freezer. We've tried preserving fillets by drying them in the sun or smoking them, but they've always gone bad within a week.

We're not the only ones to use the fish trap. One night I overslept and got down to it after all the water had drained out, to find only a scattering of silver scales and the paw marks of an otter in the sand. On another night in the torchlight I caught a glimpse of a brown shape scampering away over the rocks, and found on the sand a large sea trout, half-eaten from the head. We ate the rest for breakfast, which seemed a fair division of the spoils. I've spent many twilight hours trying to catch sea trout on a fly, but I've only succeeded once, when I hooked a two-pounder in the shallows just off the mouth of a burn. Otherwise the midges and the seaweed have been too much for my modest skills with a fly rod. However if you cast a spinner from the beach or from the rocks, it's quite easy to catch little trout, never more than half a pound, at any time of day.

Mackerel

If ever there was a mackerel-crowded sea, it's the water around Inninmore Island. Or so it was 40 years ago. These days the mackerel aren't so plentiful and you have to work harder for your supper. The mackerel follow the myriads of sand eels that come into the Sound in the summer. You can tell they've arrived as you walk along the path and see far out in the Sound darker patches of water the size of a tennis court and flecked with white specks, where the fry have been driven to the surface by mackerel and attracted all the gulls from miles around. Life in a shoal of sand eels, attacked from below and above, must be a miserable mixture of overcrowding and terror. Sometimes they're so frantic to escape that they fling themselves onto the rocks or into a boat. In the early days, if we wanted mackerel for supper, we would set out to catch them only an hour beforehand, so certain were we of success. On a calm day we've looked down into the water and seen vast phalanxes of the dark-backed fish, speeding and veering in unison like starlings going to roost. Today we often return empty-handed after fishing half the day. The birds are the best indicator of the presence of mackerel, some being more reliable than others. Terns are too skittish and will dive excitedly at any speck of flotsam, though if you see a tern carrying a sand eel you can get a bearing on the shoal by drawing a

line back from the island that hosts the tern colony. Herring gulls are more selective in their interest, while greater black-backed gulls and shags sit around on the surface waiting patiently. Gannets are the surest guides. They only come when there are mackerel about, perhaps three or four at a time, steadily quartering the water from 100 feet up, their rapid wing beats interspersed with glides, their gleaming whiteness putting the gulls to shame. Then, without warning, comes an abrupt vertical dive into the water that you think must break their necks. Then, half a minute later, the slow take-off into the wind like a seaplane.

We usually catch mackerel on hand lines let down over the side of the boat. As the boat drifts sideways to the wind, you can trail one line from the bows and one from the stern, hoping they won't get tangled if there are fish on both at once. We like to make our own sets of mackerel feathers, rather than using the garish colours and orange lines available in every seaside shop. Gull feathers picked up from the beach and tied to a hook with fine nylon do just as well, or better if you add a body of silver paper. When there's a breeze you need a heavy sinker to stop the line coming up to the surface as the boat drifts. We allow the line to sink a few feet at a time, with frequent upward jerks, until a slackening shows the weight is on the bottom. The process is then repeated, pulling the line up again. Getting into a shoal of mackerel is one of the few experiences guaranteed to excite people of any age and even the dourest disposition. Suddenly there's a tug, then another, and another, and within seconds the line is being pulled this way and that. As you haul the line in and wind it round its spool, one moment the resistance is almost too strong to overcome, the next moment it goes slack as the fish swim back towards you. You peer eagerly down into the water. At last you see a silver shape, twisting and diving to get away, then another, and another. You lift three gleaming fish up into the air and swing them over into the boat, where they flap around on the bottom, weaving your line into a tangle and threatening your feet with flailing hooks. You unhook the fish one by one, and if they're big enough, you kill them with a sharp blow on the head and drop them in the bucket. During all this the boat may be lurching heavily in the waves and the gulls are screaming overhead. You hurry to sort out the tangle and get your line back in the water before the shoal has moved away. I've also

caught mackerel when spinning for sea trout from the beach. They pull so fiercely that you think you've hooked a monster, only to be disappointed when a fish of modest size finally comes exhausted to the shore. Mackerel straight out of the sea are a different species from the drab corpses laid out on a fishmonger's slab: the bars on their backs are a richer hue of blue-green, their bellies are exquisitely iridescent, and they smell freshly of the ocean.

As with sea trout, there's no point in taking more than half a bucketful, because you can't eat them all before they start to stink. We've tried splitting them open and drying them in the sun, but this only pleased the bluebottles. Smoking them was more successful but laborious. Our first smoker was the ancient tin oven found in the kitchen of the big house. It had racks for the fish in the top half, and underneath a space where we put a Primus stove with a tray of sawdust over it. It took a lot of sawdust to smoke the fillets adequately, and it was hard to adjust the flame so that the sawdust smouldered rather than bursting into flames. The metal eventually rusted away, so we built a replacement out of wood. This proved to be disastrous. One afternoon we left the smoker gently smouldering while we went back out to catch more fish, and looked back to see a pall of smoke rising up as the whole contraption blazed into a pile of ash. But when it worked properly it produced a real delicacy, much juicier than the smoked mackerel in plastic packs you can buy in the shops, and with a tang of whatever wood the sawdust came from. Soused mackerel, made by soaking fillets in vinegar and herbs for 48 hours, is equally delicious, but won't keep for more than a few days

When using the mackerel feathers we often also catch what the locals call cuddy and the books call saithe or coalfish. They're usually found deeper down or by the rocks, and with their slim profile and dark olive-green backs are as handsome as mackerel in a less flashy way, Their flesh is less oily and strong than that of mackerel, and some people prefer it. On two occasions, when the feathers were near the bottom, we've caught small cod, though we've never been successful when deliberately trying to catch cod with lugworms. One November some optimistic friends who hoped to find mackerel staying late, caught instead some fish that sound like whiting, with big eyes and a thin dark line down their sides. Egg pouches thrown up on the beach proclaim the presence of dogfish, and we occasionally see them swimming in the kelp at low tide. We've caught them on a static line baited with lug worms and pegged out on the sand. With their sly little eyes, writhing bodies and rasping skin, dogfish aren't pretty to look at, but they're surprisingly good to eat.

Beach harvest

In about our fifth year at Inninmore, in the middle of a hot day in July, we heard herring gulls screaming excitedly from the beach. Herring gulls are often noisy but this was exceptional. They kept flying down to the water's edge where they seemed to be finding something very tasty. We went down to investigate. It was the lowest tide of the month and more sand than usual was exposed. The gulls flew up as we approached, but they kept flying over and chiding us for intruding on their rightful meal. Just above the water line lots of tiny fish were flipping about on top of the sand. They didn't attempt to get back to the water, but just flipped around until they were dried up in the sun, or, if we hadn't been there, were snapped up by a gull. We threw them back into the sea, but more appeared as if by magic, and we noticed them emerging from the sand one by one, first just the head, then, after a wriggle, the whole body.

sandeels

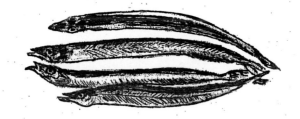

They were sand eels, and we thought they'd probably buried themselves in the sand to spawn - no species could survive such suicidal behaviour unless it had first completed its reproductive process. We ran to get a bucket, which was soon a quarter full, enough for a delicious meal of whitebait. In subsequent summers, for the children collecting sand eels was one of the high spots of the visit. It's an ideal form of fishing for a toddler: no boat, no hook, no need for grown-up help, and guaranteed success. But it only happened on two or three days in mid-July when the tide was lowest. You didn't have to go and look because the gulls would always tell you. Today sand eels are far less plentiful; we've not had whitebait for several years now, and the birds that feed on them are all much scarcer too.

The bases of the rocks around the fish trap are coated in mussels, mainly rather small, but some big enough to eat. You can pick a potful in half an hour, but you have to leave them to soak in the burn overnight to get rid of the grit, though a few tiny pearls may be left. We often find a pile of empty mussel shells carelessly thrown into the bushes outside the cottage by a previous visitor. There are also some cockles in the sand in the sump of the fish trap, but they're much less plentiful and it takes half a day to gather enough for a meal. In contrast there are tens of thousands of little winkles among the seaweed, in every shade of brown and green. They're delicious with a touch of Marmite, but you need a lot of patience to accumulate a decent mouthful. Like elephants, winkles seem to have a traditional graveyard where they go to die, and there's one spot among the rocks where you'll always find a pile of empty shells, multi-coloured and lovelier in death than in life.

We find the shells of scallops on the beach, and scuba divers sometimes come to hunt for them out in the bay. Sadly this is not one of our skills, and although the White House restaurant in Lochaline serves the best dish of scallops in the world, we've never had any to eat at Inninmore. Local fisherman put down creels in the bay to catch large prawns, and once or twice I've gone out in the boat when the creels are being lifted and come back with a bucket full of prawns waving their feelers in futile protest. They're greeted with delight by the adults, who lick their lips and look for the garlic, but not by the children, who want to put the poor creatures back in the sea.

We've tried to catch crabs and lobsters in various models of home-made creel, baited with mackerel or a meat bone or half a tin of bully beef, and lowered on a rope with a marker in different parts of the bay. At first it was always exciting as you hauled the creel up from the bottom, but we never had any success, catching no lobsters and only the wrong sort of crab. Our only edible catch has been the occasional dogfish and numerous whelks, rubbery and flavourless when cooked, and we soon gave up trying. We sometimes find little flounders in the fish trap, even during the day. They wriggle down in the sand as the water gets lower, with just their knobbly heads protruding, and you may have to locate them with your toes. Some are big enough to eat, but their flavour is so delicate that you need to clean the frying pan thoroughly and cook them on their own.

Recreation

For me staring out of the window or wandering down the beach are recreation enough, but the children sometimes say that they need other things to do. During the day there are favourite expeditions. We go to the island for a picnic. It has to be fairly calm or we can't land safely on the rocks, and we have to allow for the tide when we tie up the dinghy. As we approach the seals flop into the sea and inspect us, while the gulls, whose noise and smelly habits can make the place rather unattractive, scream their objections from above. The middle of the island is covered with impenetrable scrub, but we can get the whole way round on the rocks that rise abruptly from the sea.   The rocks are decorated by brilliant lichens, some in flat patches of chrome yellow, some in little tufts of turquoise, interspersed with cushions of pink thrift. In the spring, in the days when the gull colony still thrived, we'd come across numerous clutches of beautiful eggs or newly hatched chicks, which, as they grew bigger, would creep off into the scrub to hide from their wicked uncles, the greater black-backs.   Once, peering into the undergrowth, we found an eider duck's nest with six eggs, and the children learnt how an eiderdown got its name. We watch a trawler going past and wave at the fishermen, who wave back. It always seems to be windy on the island and we begin to feel cold. We find a sheltered spot, kindle a little fire with dried grass, nourish it with driftwood and heat a can of baked beans. Then I start worrying about the dinghy, and we clamber back over the rocks to see if it's drifted away. The island is a good place for a picnic but a bad place to be marooned.

Or we may decide to have our picnic on the Table of Lorne, which is a slab of basalt near the summit of the hill behind the cottage. The children say that if it's a table we must take a tablecloth. We laboriously climb up the hillside, zigzagging from side to side and pausing frequently to get our breath and admire the view, taking care that the tussock we've chosen to sit on isn't an ants' nest. At first the adults complain about the hard going and the children show off their energy. When the children start to flag, it's the adults who are cheerful and say it'll be easier in a moment. When we reach the crest of the cliff we start the long slog up the tussocky slope to the summit. At last we're there, and fling ourselves on the ground to recover, complaints banished by the achievement. It's a clear day, and we survey the world around us like so many eagles. To our south the Sound of Mull stretches itself majestically across the panorama, to the right disappearing among the distant hills, to the left bending away southwards to become the Firth of Lorne. From this point the cottage and the island are hidden beneath the cliffs, but across the Sound we can make out all the shops along the straggling main street of Craignure. To the south-east Lismore Island lies like a dark tongue in the mouth of Loch Linnhe, the lighthouse projecting like a stud at its tip. On the coast behind the lighthouse we can see the glinting roofs of Oban. Way to the north, across the intervening hills we can just make out the jagged silhouette of the Cuillins on Skye. Close by, to the north-east a steep escarpment drops down to a large African-looking plain, where you expect to see a herd of grazing wildebeeste. In the far distance the snow-capped peak of Kilimanjaro is just visible above the haze – or perhaps it may be Ben Nevis. We lay out the tablecloth and eat our sandwiches. We go back via the helter-skelter, a sheep track that spirals down a pinnacle of rock to give a short cut down the cliff. It's very steep, but the children can manage it so long as they don't look down. The surface is loose with stones and we have to resort to sliding. We arrive back at the cottage with trousers torn and smelling of sheep.

The best time to play Inninmore Pooh-sticks is at low tide after heavy rain. We each choose a small piece of wood as a boat, and on the count of three we all throw them into the burn at the starting line, close to the cottage where we go for water. Our boats bob away downstream, dodging the rocks as they're swept under the plank bridge, between the alder bushes and through the gorse, then out onto the open stretch that runs across the beach to the sea, a distance of about 100 yards when the tide's out. The first to reach the sea is the winner. There are many hazards. A boat may get thrown onto the edge or onto a rock. It may get jammed between two stones or become snagged by weed. Or it may be caught in a whirlpool, where it looks as though it intends to gyrate forever. In any of these events the owner is entitled to pick his boat up, wait for ten seconds, and throw it back at the same level as it was stranded. The ten seconds are counted out at a furious pace and the returning throw somehow goes well downstream. Sometimes a boat disappears completely under the bank, and sometimes ownership of the leading craft becomes a matter of dispute. Throughout the race there's a clamour of exhortations, yells of triumph and shrieks of complaint. Every contestant is convinced, if luck hadn't been against him and the others hadn't cheated, he'd have won by miles.

On some visits the byre becomes a building shed for toy boats. The most seaworthy craft are made from the ends of timbers left over from the roof joists. The blocks have to be cut to the desired length, then chopped, carved, filed and sanded to form a smooth hull. Little bits of lead sheeting (left over from the skylight flashing) are nailed to the bottom in such a way as to ensure the boat floats evenly and at the right depth. The masts, with sails attached, are the tail feathers of gulls set into holes drilled into the deck. The rudder is piece of tin hinged on a nail. Launching is an anxious moment for any boat-builder. If the breeze is off the sea the boat keeps coming back onto the shingle to lie stricken on its side, but if it's caught by a puff off the land it bobs bravely out into the bay and is soon out of sight among the waves. We're left torn between pride that the craft we've built can tackle the high sea and disappointment at seeing our morning's work disappear so rapidly.

As the children grew bigger they were able to enjoy messing about in real boats, albeit little ones. Wearing a life jacket was one of the few absolute rules of the place. On a calm day they could paddle out in the small dinghy we kept to get to the mooring, or in the fibreglass canoe that Richard Collins had bought second-hand. We soon discovered why the previous owners had sold it for a knock-down price: it was a slalom canoe and extremely unstable, always wanting to veer to the left. At least this meant that it was hard for small paddlers to go far before they were noticed. Boatmen (and boatwomen) under three years old were required to have a rope attached to their craft and held by an adult on the shore. Older canoeists could go out to the island (and even go round it so long as they went anti-clockwise), pausing to put down a mackerel line, which, if they hooked several at once, would tow them along. When it's wet there are always card games. Over the years we must have accumulated at least a dozen packs of cards, but none of them ever seemed to be complete. It was such a relief when, as the children grew older, we were able to progress from snap to pontoon, though the matches we used as counters kept falling through the cracks in the table. The cracks made up for this when the divisions they made took some of the guesswork out of Pelmanism. Then of course there was painting, for which there never seemed to be enough paper and someone else was always using the best brush. The best pieces of art were collages made by Celly from shells and bits of pottery found on the beach, all mounted on well-worn driftwood. One of these, depicting flowers and butterflies, hung in the bedroom for many years until it was taken away on an unauthorised and indefinite loan to a gallery elsewhere. A string of shells across the cot made a plaything that engaged little eyes and hands for many hours. There were also attempts at making pottery and models from the grey clay that can be dug from beneath the sand in the fish trap. The process, so deliciously messy, usually gave more satisfaction than the product, apart from a lovely model of a ringed plover dragging its wing, which was made by a paediatrician friend. Unfortunately we weren't able to fire it properly and after a few years on display it crumbled away. Other materials available close by are withies and hazel rods, from which Heather makes trays and baskets.

I made a frame for three-dimensional noughts and crosses out of driftwood, and we collected a set of black and white pebbles from the beach as counters. We soon discovered that the hole right in the middle had to be blocked off, because whoever put a pebble there would always win the game. We used the same pebbles to play draughts on a handsome home-made chequer board. The same board was used for chess, with men painted on little cubes of wood. There was another board for snakes and ladders, annotated with gains and hazards relating to the journey to the cottage: "Outboard starts first pull" took you forward four spaces, while "Fall into a burn" took you back three. Scrabble was more popular with adults, and when it was played in dyads of parent and child to make it fairer, the adults tended to lock horns and leave the children side-lined. As the children grew older, games were less in demand and the row of paperbacks on the bookshelf in the bedroom grew longer. We set up an exchange library system by which people were encouraged to leave the book they'd brought with them and take away one they hadn't read. The result has been the survival of the tattiest – which are often also the tackiest.

Sailing

Except in a westerly gale the Sound of Mull is ideal for sailing, with great stretches of open water, few hazards, shelter never far away and wonderful scenery all around. In summer a yacht or two can almost always be seen from the cottage, either running before the wind way out in the middle, or coming diagonally towards the shore on the beat, the flap of the sails as they go about sounding like gunshot. The charts mark Inninmore Bay as an anchorage and quite often a yacht drops anchor for the night between the island and the shore. Sometimes the crew come ashore in a dinghy to stretch their legs. Most keep to themselves further down the beach, but a few come to the cottage out of curiosity. If they seem congenial we invite them in for a cup of tea, but if they appear haughty and condescending – and some yachtsmen can appear so – they're left on the doorstep with the midges. The entries in the visitor's book show that people are more likely to come when they can see the cottage is unoccupied, and that occasionally they appreciate a night spent ashore. Each July there a regatta at Tobermory, with a race round Mull as the high spot. For an hour or more the Sound is decorated with a host of sails fluttering past like butterflies, the larger yachts moving at a stately pace, the small ones scurrying to keep up. Most of the time the boats wear respectable white like cricketers, but when they turn down wind their spinnakers break out into the garish colours of footballers.

After years of watching other sailors we acquired our own sailing boat, a venerable Wayfarer with a red sail. She was ideal for the waters of the Sound, being stable enough to cope with the choppy seas but lively enough to give a good sail. At first we used to take her on her trailer right down to the beach at Inninbeg, but we had difficulty pulling her back up the steep track when it was wet, so we switched to launching her from one of the jetties on the side of Loch Aline. Our carload had to split into two, one party going in the Wayfarer, the other in the white boat with the supplies. Arriving at Inninmore by sail on a fine day was always a magical experience. Once there we either beached the Wayfarer, repeatedly adjusting her position with the tide, which was rather a nuisance, or we left her trailing from the stern of the white boat at the mooring. This proved to be a dangerous practice, as any experienced sailor could have told us. At night you could tell that the Wayfarer was still there from the sound of her halyards slapping against her metal mast, the stronger the wind the louder the noise. One evening the Wayfarer was moored as usual with her painter made fast to the aft thwart of the white boat, the only place a rope could be attached. The westerly wind grew to a gale, and despite the shelter of the rocky promontory, both boats tossed and bucked like broncos. The tide was in and it was impossible to get to them. I went down to the beach and shone the torch on them through the rain. Both seemed secure. I went to bed, and as I lay in the darkness I was reassured to hear, through the lulls in the wind, the faint sound of the slapping halyards. I kept waking and straining my ears to check the sound was still there. I woke up again. The square of the window was now just discernible against the darkness. Thank heavens, dawn wasn't far away, and the worries of the night would become more manageable. I listened intently once more. The sound was no longer there. Pulling on sweater and wellies, I hurried down to the beach, blundering into gorse bushes in the gloom. In the torchlight I picked out the shape of the white boat, still tossing at her mooring, but the Wayfarer had disappeared. If she had broken loose, the westerly gale would have driven her across the bay and onto the rocks at the other side. I ran down the beach, fearing the worst. As I shone my torch ahead of me, I saw a familiar white shape rocking on her side at the water's edge. She had somehow managed to steer herself safely into the only patch of sand on an otherwise rocky shore, and was undamaged apart from some minor distortion of her centreboard casing. Her painter, a sturdy nylon rope more than half an inch thick, had chafed right through from rubbing back and forth on the other boat's transom. After that, until we were able to construct a second mooring, we were happy to put up with the nuisance of keeping her beached.

On a calm summer's day we practised capsizing in the bay. The water seemed icy even in July and we soon learnt how to right the boat as quickly as possible. We also learnt how rapidly the wind can spring up in the Sound. On several occasions we drifted out from the shore in almost flat calm, but once out of the shelter of the bay were soon having to lean right out, showered by spray and spilling wind to keep the boat upright, wishing we'd taken in a reef. But we had many glorious sails, over to Duart where we picnicked on the shore beneath the castle, westwards down the Sound and half way to Tobermory, and many times past Old Artornish Point and up Loch Aline to pay visits to the big house. The most exhilarating – and most frightening - sail was when I took the Wayfarer, with Nicky as crew, from Inninmore to Inninbeg in a freshening westerly wind. We were ending our stay at the cottage, and the rest of the party had gone on ahead in the white boat. When we set out the wind didn't seem strong enough to merit a reef, but we were beating against the tide and after half an hour we hadn't gone more than a third of the distance, while the wind had strengthened to about force five. It was all we could do to keep the boat upright. Our bottom halves were constantly awash and our top halves were soaked by spray. Leeway and tide made a mockery of our best efforts, and after two particularly fierce beats we were still opposite the same point on the shore. It was clear that we weren't going to make it with so much canvas. The only place we could shelter to take in a reef was back at our mooring, so I bore away and in a minute we'd planed back the distance it had taken us half an hour to beat. Normally we wouldn't have made another attempt until the wind had abated. But we had to get back to our various jobs, so we paused for a rest, reefed down the mainsail, put on the storm jib, gritted our teeth and headed out to do battle with the gale once more.

An experienced sailor would have taken it in his stride, but for
amateurs like us it was quite an experience. We found that with less
canvas we could control the boat more easily, and by spilling wind
during the puffs I could stop too much water coming over the side.
The self-bailers were life-saving. Once we were confident that we
wouldn't founder, it was just a matter of gritting it out, accepting
that we'd be totally soaked, hands smarting from hanging on to wet
ropes, bottoms sore from sliding on the gunwale, tummy muscles
aching from leaning out, and souls praying, every time we went
about, that the sheets wouldn't get snagged. I tacked as infrequently
as I dared. If we kept too long on starboard we went out into the
rougher water and it seemed a long way to swim to the shore, even
in life-jackets, and if we kept too long on port we came close to the
rocks, where the pounding waves promised rapid destruction for the
boat and a bruising for its crew. The rest of the party, long since
safely landed at Inninbeg, watched aghast as the hull of the
Wayfarer and its occupants kept disappearing from view in the
troughs of the waves, while the diminished sails lurched in the puffs
like a drunk who must surely fall over. I count it, in retrospect, as
one of the best sails of my life, but sadly Nicky hasn't wanted to go
sailing again – not because she was frightened, mind, but because
she didn't like the way the skipper shouted at her.

should have
taken a reef in

But disaster came much closer on another occasion. A doctor friend and his brother, who was a clergyman, took a party of children from a Sunday school in Newcastle to the cottage for Easter. The sea was reasonably calm when they arrived, and the clergyman was able to sail to the bay in his Enterprise dinghy. The next day was typically April, with blue skies, sun beginning to feel warm, a few puffy white clouds and a light wind from the west. The clergyman set off in the Enterprise with two girls to sail round the island. As they got out of the shelter of the bay and were rounding the western side of the island, a bigger and darker cloud moved overhead, the wind got much stronger and the waves quickly became more menacing. The clergyman was not an experienced sailor and his crew were novices, and they were now half a mile out. They tried to head back to land but they couldn't keep the dinghy balanced and she capsized. Righting an Enterprise in those circumstances was virtually impossible, so the clergyman told the girls to cling to the upturned boat while he tried to swim to the island, pulling the dinghy behind him by a rope. In the stiff breeze and steep waves it couldn't be done. The clergyman became exhausted and the boat was blown past the island and further out into the Sound.

The rest of the party watching from the shore could do nothing. It was much too far to swim out, they had no other boat and they had no means of summoning help (it was before the days of mobile phones). All they could do was go down on their knees on the shingle and pray. One of the few ships to go down the Sound that morning was a little tramp steamer called *Miracle*, on her way from Oban to the Hebrides. She was way out in the main channel, at least a mile from the stricken dinghy, but a sharp-eyed crew member happened to see the little boat capsize and got the skipper to alter course and see if help was needed. By the time they pulled the clergyman out of the water he was unconscious, while the two girls were paralysed and speechless with cold and utterly exhausted. A little longer in the water and they would all have been dead. *Miracle* wasted no time, but set off immediately for Tobermory, where the three were taken straight to the hospital. After warming up they all recovered quite quickly. However their friends on the shore, not knowing what had happened, remained distraught with anxiety for many hours until the news finally got through to them. I didn't witness these events myself but I've narrated them as faithfully as I can from the accounts of participants. On hearing the story hard-bitten sailors mutter about irresponsible seamanship, while more devout souls rejoice in the miraculous demonstration of the power of prayer. Maybe both are right.

Weather

The weather plays a big part in life at Inninmore. Rain determines whether the journey in and out, on foot or by boat, is a pleasure or a misery. Besides the unpleasantness of water trickling down your neck or filling your boots, and the hazards of slipping on wet rocks, there's the nuisance of disintegrating cardboard boxes and paper bags, and of finding the spare clothes in your pack already soaked when you want to change into something dry. Once you've got there the weather largely dictates what you do. If it's hot you can just lie on the lawn reading a book or laze around in the boat. If it's dry but cool you can go for a brisk walk up the hill or search for wood along the shore. If it's wet you may prefer to potter about in the byre or play a game indoors. The clarity of the air and the reflections from the sea make fine days at Inninmore seem finer than they do anywhere else - though in the early morning and evening midges may interfere with your appreciation. In foul weather you can get the satisfaction of the burrowing animal at being snug inside your den, protected by thick walls and overhanging eaves against the elements raging outside, body and spirit warmed by a good fire – though when you most need a fire it's most difficult to get enough dry wood to keep it going. The world you see through the window can change in a few hours from the Cote d'Azur to a gloomy Norwegian fjord as blue skies and sun give way to lowering cloud.

When the wind's in the west you get good warning of the weather coming up the Sound. You can spot a rain cloud heading your way when it's still ten miles away, measuring its progress by the rate at which the hanging curtain of rain obscures the detail on the coast of Mull. If you're out fishing you can calculate exactly when you need to head for home to avoid a soaking. On a larger scale, you're given several hours' warning of the approach of the prolonged rain of a warm front. First, the blue of the sky goes milky

and the sun seems out of focus because of diffuse cloud very high up. Then, as the wedge of cloud gets lower and thicker, the sun disappears altogether and the brightness goes out of the day. Then the wind picks up a little and cloud starts spilling over the tops of the Mull hills; then the lower slopes also disappear behind the veil of approaching rain. You feel the first light drops of rain on your cheek. You know it's time to go inside, revive the fire and settle down at the table with a book. After it's been raining steadily for several hours, you'll at last be able to make out a bright margin low down in the west as the end of the front approaches. You know that before bedtime you'll be able to walk down the beach and admire the wet pebbles glistening in the evening sun.

Local people say that Inninmore doesn't heed the general forecast but has its own peculiar weather system. This is true up to a point, for there are days when the sun shines at Inninmore when it's raining everywhere else, and other days when the reverse applies. The local differences arise from the disposition of the nearby mountains, which sometimes divert the wind a few points from its general direction or affect the formation and track of the clouds. A frequent and annoying deviation from the surrounding pattern occurs when the wind brings moist air from the south-west: Ben More, the highest peak on Mull but out of sight behind closer hills, then triggers a procession of rain-bearing clouds that pass directly overhead all day, while a little to either side there's tantalising blue sky. On other days, the standing waves generated by Ben More or other mountains may produce lenticular clouds higher up; these don't produce rain but may blot out the sun, never moving away because they're being constantly reconstituted in the same position. The Gulf Stream keeps the west coast of Scotland warm enough for semi-tropical plants to grow in sheltered gardens, but sometimes the cold can snap at you unexpectedly. There've been mornings when the cold has seeped through the bedclothes and woken us early. The insides of the windowpanes are framed with fern-like patterns of frost, and the lawn outside has turned from green to white, as if blanched by the brightness of the moon. It's your turn to light the fire. You pull on a sweater, trousers and wellies and scurry out to the woodshed, your breath condensing in visible exhalations. If you're quick the cold won't penetrate your clothes before you're back inside, but your fingers go numb as they clutch the bundle of wood. Soon flames and smoke are going up the chimney, but it seems an age before there's enough heat to thaw out your hands. You put the small kettle on the grill to make a cup of tea, and half-fill a saucepan with water and oatmeal. Porridge is the best warmer of them all. After breakfast you walk down to the beach leaving footprints in the frosty grass. The burns are lined with little shelves of ice, with curving white patterns where the air has infiltrated underneath. There are even shards of ice along the margin of the sea. As the morning progresses and the shadow of the hill moves eastwards over the meadow, the sun reclaims the grass from the moon and turns it back to green. At Bird Cherry Falls, where the winter sun can't penetrate, all through the day tapering fangs of ice hang down over the eroded orifice in the sandstone. Occasionally there are quite impressive falls of snow, and one particularly cold April some friends were able to build a snowman five feet tall.

Low clouds can form a variety of patterns in the Sound. Sometimes they make a layer above the water but below the tops of the hills, which then look as though they're floating on a sea of cloud. Sometimes the cloud sits on the surface of the sea like fog, and the ships hoot mournfully as they go slowly by, with only the tops of their masts visible. Sometimes a layer of cloud makes a dark ceiling over the middle of the Sound, while light comes in from the sides and from occasional shafts of sun, like the illumination of a giant stage. You almost expect to see a ballerina pirouetting over the water under the distant spot lights. The same little cumulus cloud can change from black to white, according to how the light falls on it and on the bank of clouds behind. Sometimes you can mistake a shaft of sunlight coming through the clouds in the distance for a rain shower, until you see that its slant doesn't correspond with the wind and there's a bright patch at its base as it traverses the sea or the hills. On a cloudy day you appreciate the subtleness of grey, a colour usually undervalued but now displayed in its infinite variety by sea and sky. The sea is metallic, predominately pewter but with inlays of silver, sometimes burnished and sometimes dull, flecked with white where wind opposes tide and stained with dark patches where the surface is ruffled by squalls. Above it, the sky has a whole spectrum of softer tones of grey, as varied as the many different species of dove, and like doves sometimes suffused with purple and mauve. When low cloud obscures the top of the cliff behind the cottage and wisps trail mysteriously down over the tree-covered slopes, it looks like the escarpment in *The Lost World* and you wouldn't be too surprised to see a pterodactyl gliding through the mist.

Once or twice each summer, when an anti-cyclone is centred overhead, the air is still and there's scarcely a cloud all day long. In the early morning the midges are terrible, but as the sun gets hotter they abruptly disappear. You sit outside and have a leisurely breakfast, knowing you won't get much done that day. By ten o'clock the gorse bushes along the shore are starting to wobble in a heat haze, and all the gulls are paddling in the shallows. The cliff face to the north-west warms up and radiates extra heat into the bay. Except where the tide slides lazily past the island, the surface of the sea is absolutely smooth, as though an army of laundresses had come and ironed out all the wrinkles in the night. As you walk down the beach at high tide you can see the bank of granite pebbles slanting away underwater, their colours brighter than on land, and if you go out in the boat you can see the forest of seaweed far below, each frond standing upright and still.

August '98.

You hear the throb of a marine engine long before a ship comes into view, and long after it has disappeared you can follow its wake progressing along the distant shore. You can hear a fish jump or a porpoise blow a mile away, and you can spot the ruffled circle of a mackerel strike half a league down the Sound. You watch a piece of wood drifting westwards on the incoming tide, and you see the same piece drift back along the same track later in the day. It's too hot to work. You sit on the lawn and read a book but get driven indoors by horseflies. A few brave souls go down to the sea for a swim. Those who prefer a warm shower can put water in a black plastic bag (you can buy one designed for the purpose) and hang it in the sun for an hour or so. After lunch your limbs, idle all morning, demand a rest, so you take a siesta, spurned on other days. At teatime it's too hot to light a fire and have a brew, so you drink water from the burn. It tastes delicious and it's hard to tell when you've had enough. In the evening the sunset seems to go on forever, and you stroll up and down the beach chatting, with the languid volubility that comes at the end of a hot day. Then, abruptly, the midges are there again.

If it's still clear at night, and there are no midges, no mist and no moon, you get as good a view of the stars as from anywhere on earth. The air is freshly cleaned by the Atlantic and there's no light pollution, not even the glow of a distant town behind the hills. The only artificial lights you can see are two orange street lamps in Craignure peeping through the declivity in the island, a few tiny points along the slopes of Mull where farmers' wives are reading late, and every three seconds a flash from the little lighthouse in the Sound, its reflection stabbing at you over the water to make an exclamation mark upside down. Up above *Venus* and *Jupiter* shine out brilliantly, as though on a collision course with the earth. You can identify numerous constellations, and you now appreciate why the ancients gave them such fanciful names. Among the most familiar is the *Plough*, its forward slash directing you to the *Pole Star*, which sits right over the cleft in the hill behind the cottage. In winter *Orion* stands out over Mull. At any season the *Milky Way* girdles the vault of the sky like a broad sash, rotating slowly through the night as the earth turns within its galaxy. Can those myriad tiny points of light really all be other suns, and might they each have planets? By comparison the satellites pursuing their steady paths across the heavens (you'll always see one if the midges allow you to wait long enough) seem paltry and mundane. Once, in October, we saw the Northern Lights, their cold and disembodied luminescence shifting to and fro above the cliffs, ethereal spirits conjured up by the roaring of the stags.

And then there are gales. You're woken by the sound of the air in the chimney vibrating like a giant organ pipe and the rhythmic crashing of the waves along the beach. In the early dawn you can just make out low clouds hurrying past from the west, surely faster than ever before, the horizontal white crests of waves in the Sound and the vertical white plumes shooting up from the rocks. You're thankful that you'd seen the signs of an approaching storm and taken the boat off her mooring the previous evening, beaching her out of the reach of the waves. Later, when you get up and go outside, the noise of the wind and sea overwhelms your senses. It's hard to pull the door shut behind you, and you taste the salt on the wind. Squalls of rain rush at you horizontally, and the firewood's soaked by the time you've carried it back from the shed. You arrange it in sequence by the fire, so that the wet bits can dry out before they need to be put on. The fire keeps puffing smoke into the room as gusts of wind deflected downwards by the cliffs hit the chimney. You can't imagine how any ships can sail on such a day, but through the curtain of rain and spray you can just make out the *Clansman* ploughing steadily into the gale en route for Tiree, pitching through thirty degrees despite her solid build. You're thankful you're not aboard but tucked up safe in your burrow. On the cliff to the west a plume of water curves upwards from a burn, as the water coming down from the hill is continually recycled by the up-draught. To stand outside you have to lean into the wind, and it's almost impossible to make headway into the gale. The trees toss their branches furiously as if trying to shake them off, and you daren't go into the wood for fear that one will fall on you. All the birds have disappeared. As the gale abates you assess the damage: two more slates off the roof, the wheelbarrow blown right across the lawn and the washing up bowl disappeared completely, a large ash tree snapped off halfway up, leaves lacerated on their branches or blown off in their prime and strewn on the ground, the burns swollen to tumultuous juggernauts gouging new channels through the meadow, and, down the beach, a wall of tangled kelp and a new crop of fishing buoys festooned across the rocks. All just because someone drew the concentric circles on the weather map more tightly than usual, and the air felt compelled to rush from one place to another to try and equalise the pressures. By evening the gulls are back, slanting down the wind as it abates. Then other creatures emerge from their burrows and life returns to normal.

Ships and aeroplanes

The Sound of Mull is on the route for ferries plying from Oban to the Hebrides, and every day several go past in either direction. They've got bigger and faster over the years, and although their cheerful Caledonian McBrayne livery makes them look like pretty toys at a distance, they seem monstrous if you're in a little boat and stray into their path. The *Isle of Mull*, which goes to Tobermory twice daily, calls in at Craignure, a village on Mull right opposite the cottage. Craignure has a grocery and, in recent years, an excellent hardware store. It's closer for shopping than anywhere on the mainland, and when we have the boat we often cross over the Sound to get provisions. We've learnt to scan the horizon to the east to see if the *Isle of Mull* is approaching. A tiny shape in the distance can grow within a few minutes to a huge shape bearing down on you with a momentum that seems to make collision inevitable. How can her helmsman, so high up and remote, possibly notice our little boat? And if he did, would he heed the rule that steam gives way to sail? At last she starts to curve away and turn in towards the jetty. We resume our course for the old stone pier, tossing and rocking in her bow wave.

The Sound provides a relatively sheltered passage for ships sailing up or down the west coast, and its main channel is deep enough to take the largest vessels – indeed Loch Linnhe, just round the corner, which forms part of the great geological rift across Scotland, has some of the deepest water round the British Isles and was used for dumping surplus shells after the First World War. Besides the regular ferries we've seen almost every type of boat go past: deep sea trawlers, ocean-going tugs, all sorts of warships, including submarines, cruise liners, tankers, Trinity House vessels, bulk carriers, huge floating cranes, and even the royal yacht

Britannia. One nautical enthusiast who stayed at the cottage wrote in the visitor's book that seeing all the ships go by was the most enjoyable thing about his visit.

Faslane is not far down the coast, and in the early days of nuclear submarines they sometimes came through the Sound. The first time one passed it was a while before we realised what it was and we nearly came to grief as a result. We were out in the old grey boat collecting firewood from along the shore. It was a calm day and there were no waves, so I'd carelessly left the boat anchored in very shallow water a foot or so above the rocky bottom, while we waded in and out carrying pieces of driftwood. After a while we noticed a large dark shape, like a square black sail, approaching from way down the Sound to the west. As it got closer, which it did much too rapidly for a sailing ship, we could make out a curious lump in the sea ahead of it. Then we realised that the dark shape was the conning tower of a huge submarine and the lump was the water displaced by the submerged hull ahead of it. As it went by we could see men standing on the tower, which fully deserved the name, and a white ensign fluttering horizontally, such was the speed of the boat. The water didn't break at the bows, but simply rose up over the hull in a smooth mass, as though a whale was about to surface. It was a menacing sight, in keeping with its awesome powers. The submarine soon disappeared eastwards behind the island and we resumed our wood carrying. After a few minutes I heard a whooshing sound, out of keeping with the stillness of the day, and looked up to see a wall of water approaching the shore like a tsunami. We'd forgotten the bow wave, which had been steadily advancing towards us from the centre of the channel a mile or so away. I just had time to rush splashing out to the boat, heave the anchor on board, free the rowlocks and oars from the wood piled on top of them, and row twenty frantic strokes to get her into deeper water. Then the wave picked the boat up four feet and dumped her down again as far below the former surface. If I hadn't moved her the old wooden hull would have been smashed to pieces. We haven't seen any nuclear submarines since that first year, and I wonder if they had to stop going down enclosed waterways because the navy found itself paying out too much in compensation for smashed boats.

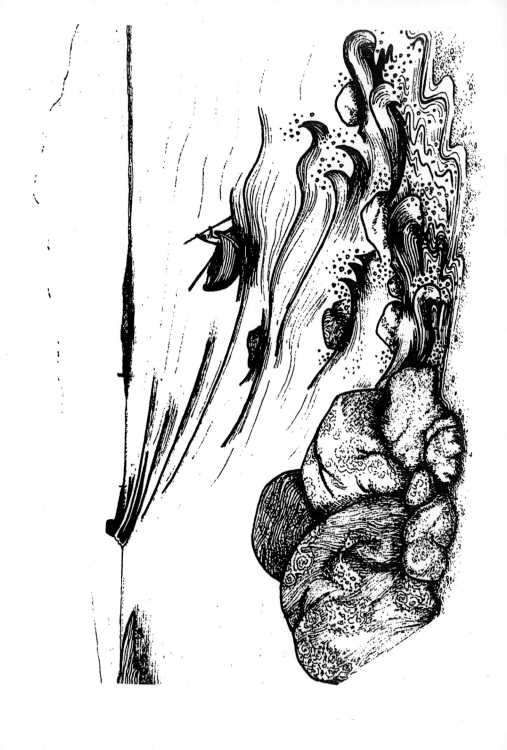

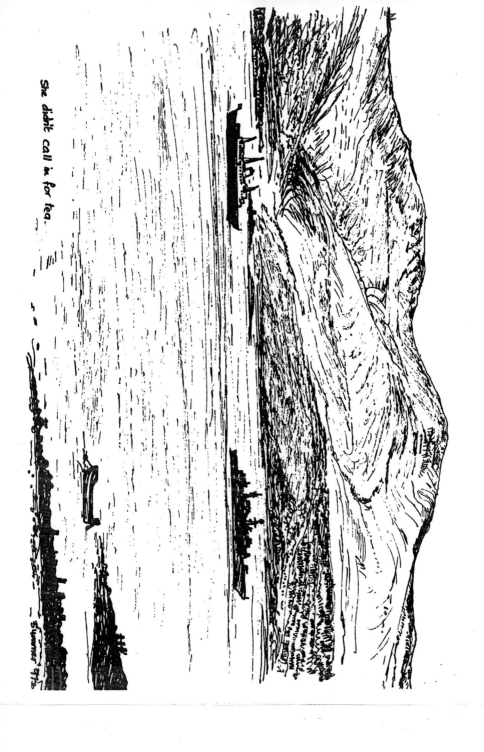

She didn't call in for tea.

— Summer '73

In 1987 a granite quarry was opened at Glensanda some six miles up the shore of Loch Linnhe. The site was chosen partly because the depth of the water allowed huge bulk carriers to tie up and be loaded by a chute. Unbelievably powerful machines have since crunched a vast bite into the hillside, while the chewed up granite has been taken away to build roads all over the world – though ironically there's still no road to Glensanda and everything has to come in by sea. These bulk carriers are the biggest vessels that pass by the cottage. They announce their approach with repeated blasts on a horn of basso profundo, then pass majestically behind the island, superstructure obscured when they're laden but showing above the skyline when they're empty, and the bows emerging at one end of the island just as the stern is disappearing behind the other. Some of the cruise liners that pass down the Sound are almost as big, looking all the bigger because of their brilliant white paint by day and their brilliant illuminations at night. Occasionally one anchors for the night near Craignure, an island of opulence floating off a barren shore.

Britannia came past on her last voyage as the royal yacht. We were alerted to her approach by the sound of cannon fire from the south-east: Lady Maclean at Duart Castle was saluting her friend the Queen Mother as she passed. First to appear was a sleek grey escorting warship, from which high-speed inflatables buzzed like bees, checking for potential attackers along the route (it was a time of frequent and unpredictable IRA attacks). One of these little craft came speeding into our bay to inspect us and our boat, and when the two desperados on board (I think they were from the Special Boat Squadron) had assured themselves we were harmless, they sped away towards Old Ardtornish. Lady Maclean had been lucky to get away with her cannons. Then *Britannia* herself came into view, looking suitably stately and regal, much bigger than one would expect for a "yacht". We inspected her through binoculars but we couldn't see the Queen, a disappointment to the children who'd hoped to invite her for tea and scones on the lawn.

From about the early 1960s improvements in ground-to-air missiles made high flying over enemy territory too dangerous, and all RAF pilots were trained to fly low enough to be undetectable by radar. Most pilots welcomed this because it made flying more fun, though there was less opportunity to relax. Areas for practising low flying were designated all over the country; one of these was in the western highlands and included the Sound of Mull. If you'd been a Russian spy trying to find out what planes the RAF was using, you couldn't have done much better than sit outside our cottage and watch them all fly past. In the 1970s it was Hunters, Canberras and Sea Vixens, then Phantoms, Jaguars and Buccaneers, plus some larger aircraft such as Hercules' and Vulcans, and in more recent times Tornados, some with Dutch or German markings, with guest appearances by American F-16s and F-18s. The fighters come speeding down the Sound at 200 feet, so fast that by the time you hear them they're almost out of sight, and usually you can only look up in time to see the second of a pair. Or they may engage in mock combat between the hills, the roar of their engines echoing all around, and you wonder why there aren't more crashes. The Vulcans were particularly spectacular. With their huge delta-shaped wing they were designed to fly at very high altitude, but when this became impossible their strong frame enabled them to convert to low-level flight, despite the denser air and greater stresses. Unlike the fighters, which used to fly from east to west down the Sound in pairs, the Vulcans came one at a time from the south. If you happened to be looking in the right direction at the right moment, you might see one approaching, head on and silent, just above the shoulder of the Mull hills. When it reached the Sound it would drop down low over the water, then ease up again to clear the cliff at the back of the cottage. You felt the roar of its engines in your stomach and the huge shape blotted out the sun. It must have dented the ego of the eagles.

In about 1987 I was visiting the big house for dinner. A fellow guest was a young man from Suffolk who was friendly with some American pilots stationed at Bentwaters. They flew F-111s and had just carried out the raid on Colonel Gadafi's tent in the Libyan desert, an incident of shameful illegality but aeronautical brilliance. After a few beers one of the pilots had accepted a challenge from the young man to fly low over the big house at Ardtornish at precisely 8 pm on his last day there. It was a fine evening, and shortly before eight we were persuaded to go down to the head of the loch to watch the plane fly over. Five minutes went by and we became increasingly sceptical. With half a minute to go we could bear the midges no longer and turned back towards the house. The young man lingered, disappointed and embarrassed. Ten seconds to go. "Look, everybody," he shouted. Out over the Sound, about fifty feet above the water, we could just make out a small dot that quickly turned into a dark shape. Its rapid enlargement showed it must be heading straight towards us and going very fast. Eerily silent it passed through the mouth of the loch and sped between the woods on either side. Then suddenly it was right overhead, with a shattering roar of accumulated sound. We could now see that it was an F- 111, still painted in desert khaki. Just above the house it pulled up into a near-vertical climb, revealing two fiery apertures as the afterburners flamed in the exhausts, and diminished to a dot again as quickly as it had just grown. It was a brilliant display of precision flying that must have cost the American taxpayer tens of thousands of dollars.

Fire

Every year more and more rubbish gets washed up on the beach at Inninmore, and each spring, mindful of Aunt Emmeline's injunction, we collect it into piles and burn it. Plastic waste seems particularly ugly and offensive. We get the now universal detritus of plastic bags and bottles, and the fish farms down the Sound add tangles of rope, netting and food sacks. The burning plastic emits black and poisonous-smelling fumes, but there's too much of it to bin and take away. And it's more fun to burn it, especially on a cold morning. When John was eight we took him and a school friend to the cottage for the Easter holidays. An anticyclone had brought cold dry winds from the east for almost a month, and the brown tops of the grass in the meadow by the beach were tinder dry, though the ground underneath still squelched from the winter's rain. The boys helped me gather the rubbish into piles at the high tide mark and set it alight. Little outriders of flame crept outwards from the main fire through the dried seaweed and twigs on the pebbles around it, sometimes sputtering on for several feet before they petered out. I went back to the cottage to have a coffee, leaving the boys to tend the fires. After a while they shouted to me to come and look. A little posse of flames had managed to get right up to the meadow at the top of the beach, and was beginning to spread into the dead

Easter Saturday Afternoon

bracken at the edge of the meadow. I wasn't too concerned because I was glad to see the bracken burnt and I was sure the fire would go out when it reached the boggy stretch beyond. I told the boys not to worry and went back to my coffee. Soon there were more shouts and much waving of arms. I ran back down the beach to find that the fire had raced through the dried stalks above the bog and was now beginning to spread out up the slope at the back of the meadow. I'd badly misjudged the situation, but I thought we'd still be able to put out the fire if we acted quickly. The three of us stamped on the advancing flames with our boots and beat at them with sticks, deliberation turning to panic as the leading edge of fire spread ever upwards and outwards like an opening fan, driven by the brisk easterly breeze. Dread engulfed me as I realised I'd committed the unforgivable sin of starting a hill fire and it was now out of control. I ran back to the cottage and phoned the estate. Now that the fire was well established I could see no reason why it should ever stop, and I was afraid it would march on over the hills to the forestry plantations beyond and to the little settlement of houses on the western shore of Loch Sunart. Adrenalin even conjured a vision of its sweeping onwards until it reached the North Sea and of my going down in history as the man who destroyed the best part of Scotland.

Over the phone Faith didn't seem too concerned. She said that in the old days they used to burn off stretches of the hill deliberately to improve the quality of the grass. But they wouldn't have done it when it was so dry and windy. I ran back up the hillside with a spade to beat the flames more effectively, but I soon had to give up. I couldn't get close enough to the advancing front from behind because my boots got too hot, and ahead of it I had to keep retreating, fearful that I might twist an ankle in a hollow and be caught in the flames. Besides its rapid advance forwards, the fire was also spreading sideways and creeping slowly backwards into the wind. If this continued it would eventually get to the cottage. We could keep ourselves safe by going out onto the rocky promontory, where the smoke wouldn't reach us, so the best thing we could do was put all our efforts into saving the cottage. Armed with choppers, sickles and spades we set about clearing the bramble thicket at the back of the cottage so as to make a fire break. At least the building hadn't got a thatched roof and wouldn't be at risk from sparks. Adam Nicolson chose that morning to pay us a visit, and saw the smoke as he walked along the path. He enthusiastically joined in cutting the brambles, and we worked together without a pause until we'd made a clear patch as wide as a cricket pitch, lighting little controlled bonfires to consume what we'd cut so as to leave nothing for the wild fire to feed on. Scratches and pricks, normally the cause of much grumbling, went as unnoticed as small wounds in a battle. Adam was later rewarded for his labours when his piece about our fire was published in the Sunday Telegraph.

By now the smoke from the hill was visible from miles around, and someone on Mull reported it to the fire brigade at their base in Fort William. I'm told that they turned out in full uniform and helmets, and at top speed drove the 40 miles to Loch Aline, ringing their bell on the narrow roads and jumping the queue at the Corran ferry. The gleaming machine then bumped down the track to the steading at Old Ardtornish, where it could go no further. The firemen could see the smoke rising up above the cliffs three miles to the east. There was no way they could get their machine anywhere near the fire, so they had no option but to return all the way they had come, with less haste and noise, back to their base in Fort William. Meanwhile Faith had asked the Forestry Commission about the possibility of using a helicopter to douse the flames from the air. She was told that the charge would be £700 an hour, and that there was only one helicopter and she would be sixth on the waiting list because fires had been reported in several other places too. The conditions were exceptionally conducive to hill fires in the Highlands because the new grass and heather hadn't yet grown up and the old growth, still exposed, had been dried to tinder by a month of desiccating wind. This wind was still blowing and could quickly fan a single flame into a conflagration.

By evening the fire had swept over all of the hillside visible to the east, converting the brown to black, except where grey patches of granite preserved their previous colour. The flames rushed through the tops of the grass so quickly that bushes and little trees were scarcely damaged by their passage, the ground beneath being too wet to support a more solidly-based conflagration. The advancing front of the fire was now up on the tops and out of our sight, but we could still see the flames at each flank creeping outwards more slowly, towards the promontory jutting into the Sound on the east, and towards the course of the burn behind the cottage on the west. As darkness began to fall the skyline was silhouetted against the glow beyond, and clouds of orange smoke billowed up into the night sky. The eastern promontory was now ablaze throughout its length to the tip of the crocodile's snout, and the whole fiery head was reflected in the waters of the bay. It was an apocalyptic sight, which I would have thoroughly enjoyed if I hadn't felt so guilty. Meanwhile the boys were noisy and subdued alternately as excitement and fear jostled for their mood. They had already packed up their rucksacks in case a quick escape was needed.

My main concern now was that the fire would somehow cross the burn and start advancing westwards across the hillside and into the woodland towards Inninbeg. The open slopes were clothed in dead bracken, which the flames would relish, and once they'd reached the wood they would take a strong hold on the carpet of twigs and fallen trees. I took a spade and patrolled up and down the line of the burn, determined to beat back any incursion across it. The burn was only three or four feet wide, so that sparks could easily fly across, and fallen branches and bramble stalks lay across it, providing numerous crossing points for the flames. I thought of the Germans defending the Rhine against parachutists and improvised bridges, hoping my campaign would be more successful. I didn't need a torch because the whole scene was lit like a battlefield. The fire crept steadily towards me in a wavering line. Fortunately the wind dropped as night came on, and the sparks tended to go straight upwards and burn themselves out by the time they came down. Now the forward columns of the advance began to reach the edge of the burn. Brambles burnt the most brightly of all, and one after the other their stalks blazed up in a series of little flaming hoops. In places the flames started to cross, but I was always able to beat them down before they reached the other side. Bit by bit the margin of the burn had all been burnt; once it had turned black and inert it was no longer a threat. I prayed that the line was being held in the stretches higher up, where I couldn't defend. In the early hours I felt that I'd won that phase of the battle and I went back to the cottage to rest, my face fiery as if from sunburn.

The weather was still clear in the morning, and we were relieved to see the bracken on the western hillside its usual spring shade of brown, glowing in the oblique early sun. The line of the burn made a sharp demarcation from the blackened waste on the other side. We could still see billows of smoke, now white rather than orange, rising above the skyline, but they seemed less menacing in the light of day. Adam came over to see how we were faring. Together we walked up to the tops on a reconnaissance, with me having to put in a few trots to keep up with his long strides. The burn, just a thin ribbon through the hills, had completely contained the fire's westward advance. To the east it was still burning but would be halted by Loch Linnhe. Towards the north it had been stopped either by small lochans or by the snow line beyond, the black abutting the white in brilliant contrast. In my panic of the previous day I hadn't taken into account that the east wind and cold nights had preserved the snow on the tops. Even so we calculated that I'd managed to burn well over a thousand acres, all with a single Swan Vesta. I learnt later that the keeper from the estate and two colleagues had been up on the hill very early in the morning to beat the smouldering area while dew was still retarding the flames. But when the sun and breeze came up they burst back into life. The fire began on the morning of Good Friday and lasted till Easter Monday, when the wind changed and a fine drizzle began to fall. The stench of damp ash hung in the air for several days. To my relief the long-term damage didn't turn out to be too severe. Within a month fresh grass was shooting up from the blackened earth, which the deer chose in preference to the unburnt areas, rather to the inconvenience of the keeper, who had to go further afield to carry out the annual cull. Larger saplings put out leaves again, but many of the smaller ones had probably perished. By the following year the only visible sign of the fire was the black rims to the granite outcrops where the scorched moss and lichen hadn't yet had time to regenerate.

Medical problems

People often ask what we'd do if we had a serious medical emergency while we were staying at Inninmore. The question was more worrying in the early days before mobile phones were invented. Chubby tells the story of a shepherd getting on in years who had a stroke while on the hill above Inninmore and had to wait many hours before he was laboriously carried to safety on a stretcher. If something similar occurred today I suppose we'd simply dial 999 and within no time a lifeboat would come surging into the bay or a helicopter would be hovering over the beach. Minor ailments and injuries we expect to deal with ourselves, and we keep a box of bandages and basic medications in the attic. Forty years ago it was quite easy for a hospital doctor to get hold of unwanted pills and injections from surplus stock in the drug cupboard of a hospital ward, and our selection included broad-spectrum antibiotics such as ampicillin and quite powerful analgesics such as pentazocine, an intravenous opiate analogue. As a paediatrician of the old-fashioned and pragmatic school I've always taken the view, with my family as well as with my NHS patients, that most acute illnesses in children will get better by themselves, except for meningitis and appendicitis. So when one of the children was ill, all I used to do was check that they didn't say "Ow" when I bent their neck forward or prodded them in the bottom right corner of their belly, then give them a double dose of paracetamol and leave them to sleep it off. Our main worry has always been accidents, such as a fall on the rocks or off the roof, near-drowning, or, worst of all, a fire started by a candle or an upset lamp that trapped children in the attic.

Our medical problems have mainly arisen on the way in or out rather than at the cottage itself. One May, when Alex was five months old, we took him on his first visit to the cottage, and a combination of unseasonal bad weather and my stupidity nearly killed him. After we'd been there a few days he developed bloody diarrhoea (something to do with the mice, perhaps), which was rather alarming, so we decided to go home earlier than planned in case it got worse. We set off back along the path with Alex in a baby-carrier on my chest. I also had a pack on my back, so I walked slowly, taking great care not to slip and crush him. The sky darkened, the wind got up and snow began to drive almost horizontally into our faces. To start with Alex cried and made a fuss, but after a while he gradually quietened down and went to sleep, apparently lulled by the movement of my walking. I reflected that this was an excellent way to carry a small child: he stayed happily asleep while I was kept nice and warm by the small body pressed against my chest. It was still snowing nearly two hours later when we got to the car, which we'd parked by the steading at Inninbeg. We took off our packs and unbuckled the baby-carrier. Alex didn't stir. He wasn't asleep, he was nearly comatose with cold. His eyes were closed, his skin was slate-grey, his breathing was shallow and his pulse was faint and slow. He felt very cool all over. We ran up the hill to the Gaskells' cottage. They'd said we could always stay there if we wanted, but we hadn't got a key and had to force a window. I climbed in, opened the front door and got a fire going. It took an hour of warming and coaxing before he would take a feed, and another two hours before his temperature felt normal. Happily he made a full recovery and the experience hasn't stopped him growing up to enjoy many more holidays in the snow.

The worst episode, or rather two episodes in one, also involved Alex when he was two years older. We were staying at the cottage with a school friend of George's, and it was planned that after a week George and I would take the friend back to the ferry where his parents would pick him up, leaving the rest of the family behind. It so happened that on the due morning Celly had a really bad tummy ache, so we changed the plan and all left together in the boat. Celly's tummy ache got worse, and by the time we got to Inninbeg she looked pale and drawn and felt faint when she stood up. The local doctor had a good reputation, but he would probably just send her on to hospital, so we thought it would save time if we went straight to Fort William. At Ardgour there was a long queue of cars waiting for the ferry, and it was plain that it would be at least an hour before we could get on (in those days the ferry was smaller and could take only about eight cars at a time). I was brought up to regard queue-jumping as a particularly heinous crime, but for once I gritted my teeth, ignored the disapproving horns and drove straight to the head of the queue. The ferryman was sympathetic and 20 minutes later, having handed the friend over to his parents, we were driving along the twisty road that runs beside Loch Linnhe to Fort William.

The Belford Hospital at Fort William is one of those small hospitals in rural areas that provide a good basic service and are much loved by the local community, but can't afford the full range of staff or equipment now expected and are therefore under constant threat of closure. We were very thankful that its casualty department had so far survived economy cuts. Celly just managed to walk in and lie down in a cubicle. A nurse took her basic details, measured her pulse and blood pressure and called the surgical house officer. He was an affable young man with the confidence that comes with the first real job after qualification. He took the usual history and did the usual examination, then turned to us brightly. "No need for admission," he said. "It's nothing to worry about, just dysmenorrhoea. It'll soon be over. All that's needed is mild analgesics. You can go back to your cottage and enjoy your holiday." "Are you sure that's all it is?" I said. "Quite sure," he replied. "There's really nothing to find. What else could it be?" As it happened Celly and I had both recently taken the exam for membership of the Royal College of Physicians, which had entailed mugging up lists of possible diagnoses for various symptoms. Among these was a list of causes for acute abdominal pain. Dysmenorrhoea was indeed among them, but further down the list came less frequent but more serious causes such as ruptured ectopic pregnancy. But the canons of medical etiquette inhibited our questioning the diagnosis we'd been given: a doctor shouldn't act as a doctor to himself or his family, and he shouldn't argue with the doctor he's gone to for advice.

Celly hobbled uncomfortably back to the car, and after replenishing our stock of paracetamol at the chemist we drove back along Loch Linnhe to the Corran side of the ferry. Again there was a queue, but this time we had to take our turn. The tide was low and it was drizzling. The children went down to the slipway in raincoats and wellies while I sat in the car with Celly. There were a number of people pottering about on the slipway as they watched the ferry manoeuvring on the far side of the loch. Suddenly there was a shout and everybody clustered at one side of the slipway, peering at something on the rocks below. I felt instant dread in my heart. Somehow I knew it was Alex. I dashed down from the car and pushed to the front of the group. Alex was spread-eagled face down on the weed-covered rocks about fifteen feet below. I scrambled down beside the slipway and picked him up. He was limp and semi-conscious, and there was a gash on his forehead about three inches long, just at the hairline. It was bleeding copiously, and, worst of all, at the base of the wound I could see something white that looked like brain. Trembling I carried the limp body back up to the slipway, pushed through the spectators and their murmurs of

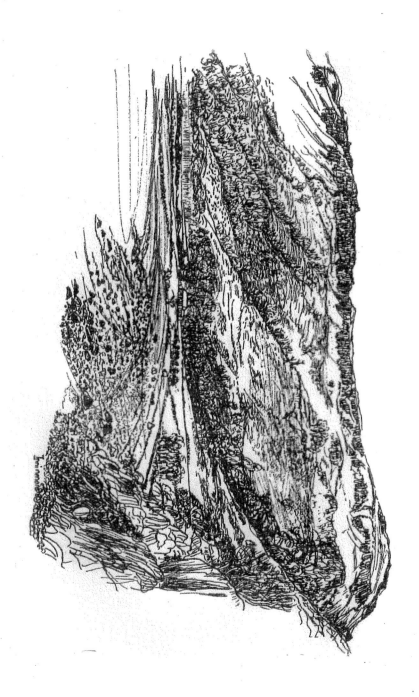

sympathy and criticism, and deposited him on Celly's lap in the passenger seat. She was feeling worse by now, and wasn't really in any state to look after him, apart from talking to him to keep him awake and pressing a hanky to the gash on his forehead - stopping the flow of blood seemed more important than the risk of infection. George and Laura sat silent in the back of the car. I drove back to Fort William as quickly as I dared. It's one of those infuriating roads with a succession of gentle bends that stop you overtaking, and holiday drivers enjoying the scenery don't take kindly to being hooted at.

At last we drove up to the hospital and I carried Alex in. He was quickly assessed and taken for X-rays. Amazingly, he hadn't fractured his skull and the white tissue I'd seen was bone rather than brain. His wound was stitched up under heavy sedation, and we were told he should stay in hospital for overnight observation. We asked if Celly could stay with him to reassure him, and she was allowed to sleep in a single room with Alex in a cot at the foot of her bed. When he was restless Celly tried to comfort him, crawling down the bed because of her pain. She then began to feel pain in her right shoulder as well, a classic symptom of blood under the diaphragm, and she called for attention. She was given something stronger for the pain, but her suggestion that she ought to have a drip up went unheeded. In the morning she was taken to the operating theatre where the consultant surgeon found three pints of blood in the peritoneal cavity and a ruptured tubal pregnancy.

Meanwhile George, Laura, and I were spending the night in a bed-and-breakfast nearby, and we only learned what had happened when we went to the hospital in the morning. Celly was still very drowsy but no longer in so much pain. She was having a blood transfusion and already looked a better colour. I spoke to the consultant, who told me he'd operated just in the nick of time. Neither of us mentioned the earlier visit to the casualty department or the long and painful night on the ward. However the house officer later had the grace to apologise to Celly for his misdiagnosis. Alex was back to normal and rather proud of the impressive bandage round his head. Later in the day the four of us went back to Ardtornish where we stayed in the big house with the Ravens for a few days, making daily visits to Fort William before driving back to Yorkshire for the beginning of term.

One of the comments I heard, and was intended to hear, while carrying Alex up the slipway was "Shouldn't have been left on his own." This criticism was unhelpful at the time but justified, and I can only plead that at that moment my attention was distracted. But even if I'd been with him he'd still have fallen, because he was under the control of a superior being. Celly's guardian angel must have given him a push. If we'd crossed back to the other side of Loch Linnhe, driven all the way back to Inninbeg and gone on down to the cottage in the boat, Celly would almost certainly have bled to death. Alex carries the angel's mark on his forehead to this day. After we'd finally got back home I wrote to thank the consultant for his skilful and truly life-saving intervention. It was the time when doctors were being forced off their pedestals and hospitals were beginning to get sued for making mistakes. Wishing to be helpful (or was it to make myself feel less guilty?) I appended a short note gently drawing his attention to the risks of leaving an inexperienced doctor in the casualty department making critical decisions without supervision. I didn't get a reply.

We didn't need to visit the Belford again until many years later, two days before Christmas. I was now with Heather, and we'd managed to persuade our two younger children aged seven and five (plus Kelly, a black Cocker spaniel), that it would be fun to forsake the television and go and spend Christmas at Inninmore. In addition to standard provisions, each of us was required to carry part of the festive fare: a chicken, a packet of stuffing, some potatoes, some Brussels sprouts, a small Christmas pudding, some tiny decorations for the tree we planned to find next day, a tin of Pedigree Chum, a bottle of coke and a bottle of wine, and a box of chocolates. Families who go on expeditions with growing children will be familiar with the ritual – and the expense – of being properly equipped. Each child has to have his or her own pack of the right size and colour and with lots of side pockets, an anorak with a hood, a woolly hat, gloves, long socks and boots. All must be new. Hand-me-downs simply won't do. After much debate the luggage was divided out and our little party set off along the path at about midday in a high spirit of adventure. We planned to have a picnic lunch en route and arrive at the cottage before it began to get dark, which would be at about four o'clock. It was a fine day and there'd been no rain for some time, so the burns were easy to cross. After a while the packs, put on so eagerly, began to get heavy and uncomfortable, and frequent rests were needed. The two small sherpas felt hot under their anoraks, which had to be taken off, which meant taking off their packs as well. As their sweat dried the sherpas felt cold again, and the anoraks had to go back on again. Bootlaces, tied with great diligence, mysteriously undid themselves. Bits of stick somehow burrowed their way down inside socks, so that boots had to be taken off and put back on, and laces tied again with the same diligence. We stopped for lunch at Picnic Rock. Kelly dashed around yelping at the unfamiliar scent of deer, and I scanned the skyline through binoculars looking for a peregrine. We hid our orange peel under a rock and set off again. Soon we were at the halfway mark, and everyone got into a routine of steady trudging, interrupted by scrambles over fallen trees. We sang a few carols, disputes over the lyrics distracting attention from aches and scratches. We had to go at the pace of the littlest, and with all our stops it was over three hours before we saw the cottage through a gap in the trees. There were excited shouts and we quickened our pace. Despite the fine weather the rocks in the shade were still wet and slippery. As we passed through Primrose Dell, the prettiest section of the path in spring, Heather's boot slipped on a slanting rock and she lurched sideways. Her pack swung her off balance and she fell, putting an arm out to save herself. She cried out and scrambled to her feet clutching her wrist. I rushed back to see what had happened. Her hand was cranked upwards in the typical dinner-fork deformity of a distal fracture of the radius and ulna.

The light was just beginning to fade, and in two hours it would be too dark to walk along the path safely, especially with the children. Should we go on to the cottage and wait till the morning before going to Fort William? If left overnight the wrist would swell up so that reduction of the fracture would be more difficult and perhaps impossible until the swelling had subsided. And until it was corrected it would be very painful. No, we had to go back straight away. I made a crude splint from a piece of wood and bound it on with spare bootlaces. We redistributed the things from Heather's pack, and I cut her a stick of hazel to steady herself – another fall would be excruciating. The children sensed the gravity of the situation and walked back the whole way back along the path, recently traversed with so many complaints, without a grumble, without a snack, and without a pause for rest. By the time we got to the car it was dark, and we needed headlights to pick our way between the potholes along the track. At Belford Hospital they were quick and efficient. Within an hour Heather had been examined and X-rayed, and the fracture was reduced under general anaesthetic. Because it was late they wanted to keep her in for observation overnight, so once again the rest of us spent the night in a bed-and-breakfast. Next morning, Christmas Eve, we went back to the hospital early to find Heather in good spirits. She was no longer in pain. Her hand, protruding below the plaster, was back to a normal posture, with very little swelling and a good circulation. I explained to the ward sister that we had a long way to go and we had to make new plans for Christmas with two small children, so we'd like to set off for home as soon as possible. I pointed out that I was a doctor. I could see that the treatment had been first-class and the result excellent. I would keep checking the circulation regularly. Could Heather be discharged straight away? But I evidently didn't press the right buttons. She replied in that unanswerable tone that God gives only to ward sisters: "If you're in the medical profession you should know that patients cannot be discharged until they've been seen by the doctor. The doctor will start his round at approximately half past eleven, if he's not delayed by more serious cases. He will begin at bed number one and will work his way round the ward to bed number thirty. Your wife is in bed number twenty-nine." Heather got dressed, I signed the necessary papers, and we walked out. Before we set off home I went into the town to buy a box of chocolates for the nurses and a colourful card with the inscription "To my Favourite Sister, wishing you a very Happy Christmas."

Chapter Three: the natural world

Eagles

It was an eagle that first led me to Inninmore, and eagles have been an important theme in our life there ever since. For as long as anyone can remember there has been an eyrie on the basalt escarpment to the north-west of the bay. The exact location has now changed, but for many years it was beneath the crag that juts out at the western end of the cliff. It was on a ledge under an overhang and couldn't be seen from above, but the heap of sticks was visible through binoculars from the front lawn of the cottage, almost half a mile away. It could only have been reached by a difficult abseil, but so far as I'm aware no one ever attempted it. Besides its inaccessibility, an eyrie at this site had the advantages of superb visibility, reliable upcurrents for soaring, and a good supply of food from the rabbits and gull chicks on the island across the bay.

Elsewhere in Scotland, if you see what you think might be an eagle, you have to ask yourself if it's really a buzzard closer to. But at Inninmore it will always be an eagle: it's eagle territory and buzzards don't dare to trespass. At any time of year, if you keep a steady watch, it won't be long before you see one, or sometimes the pair, or occasionally, when their chick is with them, all three together. Among birds that soar eagles are the effortless champions. They can glide for half the morning back and forth along the cliffs with scarcely a wing beat, or gyrate slowly in wide lazy sweeps in a thermal, getting steadily smaller with each sweep until they merge with the specks of dust in your binoculars. In early spring the male puts on a flying display past the cliffs where his mate is sitting, swooping down with wings furled, then rising up almost to the vertical, hanging momentarily in a stall, then swooping down to make another mighty loop, each swoop covering several hundred yards. Eventually he may settle on the edge of the cliff, and because we are familiar with every detail of its contours, we can often pick out the small new projection made by his silhouette - though sometimes, when we focus the binoculars, we find it's just a sheep.

Buzzards may keep away, but ravens aren't so easily scared. They don't nest on this cliff, but go past it from time to time, not at all put out by the regal residents. No mean fliers themselves, they may linger and provoke an aerial combat, using their agility to harry the eagles from above and below. The eagles affect not to notice, but when a raven comes in too close they roll sideways and present their talons to the attacker. Hooded crows may also try and harass an eagle, but with less persistence, and even kestrels, tiny by comparison but indomitable in spirit, will swoop down at one like fighters round a heavy bomber. Meanwhile herring gulls and black backs, which often fly sedately past the cliff in twos and threes, continue on their way unmolested, enjoying the respect reserved for the seafarer.

Golden eagles nest early, and by May we can usually hear the chick calling for attention. The cheeping echoes round the cliffs and can be heard from half a mile away, a surprisingly high-pitched and plaintive noise for a creature that will soon be so majestic and so silent – and may recently have murdered and eaten its brother. We often see the parents bringing food, but its shape is so distorted in their talons that we can't usually tell what it is. However we can be sure that rabbits and gull chicks from the island are – or used to be - a regular feature on the menu.

cliffs
and
waterfall

We hear a sudden commotion from the island, and look out to see a crowd of agitated gulls flying urgently upwards towards a dark shape that hovers in the sky several hundred feet above. The shape comes lower and hovers again, ignoring the gulls now swarming around it like angry bees. With a final swoop it disappears below the hillocks, and the commotion subsides. After a few minutes the noise starts up again, and the eagle can be seen flying low over the water back to the mainland, a bundle dangling from its talons and a posse of frantic gulls in pursuit. This doesn't happen any more because in the last ten years all the rabbits and nearly all the gulls have gone from the island. We're not certain why, but mink, which have been spreading along the west coast of the Highlands at the same time, are the main suspects. Although each spring ewes have their lambs in the meadows by the cottage, we've never seen the eagles come down for prey that close, and when they fly over they take care to be well above the range of a shotgun. But when we first took George to the cottage at the age of six weeks, we didn't dare to leave him unattended on the rug outside the door. Being carried away to be nourished by eagles may be a suitable exploit for a Greek demi-god, but not, we thought, for our little boy.

For the last five years, although we often still see them soaring over the cliff, the eagles haven't nested at Inninmore. We wonder if this results from the advent of their larger cousins, sea eagles. After being persecuted almost to extinction in the 19th century, sea eagles were re-introduced to Scotland between 1975 and 1985, when a large number of young birds were brought from Norway to the island of Rum. They bred successfully and began to spread to the surrounding islands, especially Skye and Mull. Occasional birds would wander across the Sound and be seen over the mainland, until in the last few years a pair has started to nest at an undisclosed site in Morvern. We now see one or two birds on most of our visits. They can't possibly be mistaken for anything else, with their lumbering flight, often at lower altitude than a golden eagle, and their huge rectangular wings, aptly compared to barn doors, which you imagine you could hear creaking if you were close enough. There are reports of sea eagles and golden eagles vying for territory, and we wonder if the latter have now been driven away from their long-standing eyrie at Innnimore. Not long ago I looked up to see the closing stages of an encounter over the cliffs. A golden eagle and a sea eagle were tumbling downwards out of the sky with their talons locked together. They soon parted and flew away in opposite directions, the golden eagle inland, the sea eagle out over the Sound. This particular encounter appeared inconclusive, but it must be unsettling for the golden eagles to have such formidable rivals frequently passing so close to their eyrie. If the golden eagles have indeed been driven away, I rather wish the sea eagles had stayed in Norway.

Other birds

We've now seen over a hundred different species while staying at Inninmore. It would be tedious to list them all, but birds are an important part of our lives there and it would leave a gap if I didn't describe the ones that feature most. When we arrive by boat in early summer our first job, like sappers marking mines in Normandy, is to mark the ringed plovers' nests on the beach so that they don't get stepped on,.

ringed plover family

They lay their eggs among pebbles of the same size, and it's extraordinarily difficult to see them even at close range. The best method is to sit quietly 50 yards away and watch the female return to incubate, though you need to be patient while she first makes numerous diversionary runs. Once located, the nest is marked with a stick and everybody keeps clear. There are usually four or five pairs of ringed plover along the beach, each standing on sentry duty to guard its territory, then dashing off to confront its neighbour, legs moving so fast you can't see them, or flying stiffed-winged a foot above the water. They're experts at leading you away from their eggs, keeping 20 yards ahead as you walk down the beach, then, when you're well past the danger area, flying in a wide sweep round behind you again. When they have chicks, little fluffy balls on legs, they may add to the deception by feigning injury, dragging a wing to entice you on. Their eye behind its bandit mask suggests a sharp intelligence, and it's hard to believe this behaviour arises merely from the mechanics of evolution and not from calculated stratagem.

Our other main shore birds, oyster catchers, don't seem to have quite the same intelligence. Their flamboyant colours, constant cheerful piping clamour and foolish demeanour make them the clowns of the beach, and they add a welcome lighter-hearted tone. They too lay their eggs among the stones, and when disturbed creep back so cautiously you often get too cold to go on watching. Or sometimes you can locate the bird sitting on its nest by scanning the stony part of the beach through binoculars and spotting a little patch of intense black and brilliant orange. The plovers always lay just above the highest tide line, but oyster catchers sometimes miscalculate and lay above the level of the neaps but below the level of the springs, so that when the tide get bigger the eggs are lethally chilled. Once I moved a clutch some five feet up the beach to safety, and was delighted when the bird came back to them and hatched three chicks successfully - human interference doesn't usually work so well. The oyster catchers like to rest on the furthest rock of the promontory that forms the western flank of the bay, a club they share happily with curlews, gulls, shags and a heron – though when an otter comes they all fly off. The pecking order on this rock is surprising. You might expect that the heron, with its lethal beak, would reign supreme, but even the heron is forced to yield to that master bully, the greater black-backed gull.

Inninmore Island lies about half a mile from the mainland and shelters the bay from the south. Until the mink arrived some 15 years ago, the island supported a large colony of herring gulls and lesser black backs, probably more than 150 pairs in all. During spring and summer you'd always be aware of their presence, because of the cloud of birds that continually hung over the island like midges, and because of the noise that kept rising to cacophonous crescendos whenever there was a quarrel or a threat. Each evening you could lie in bed with the window open listening to a concerto for two woodwinds - oyster catcher and sandpiper - and a background orchestra of gulls. The gulls, good socialists as they are, all start laying on 1st May, a date well known to local trawlermen, who used to pause at the island on their way back to Oban and pick up some eggs. The gulls were so plentiful that a modest harvesting of eggs made little difference, and we too joined in whenever we were there at the right time and the water was calm enough to go across to the island in the dinghy. The eggs are very beautiful, with their tapering shape, green background and blotchy brown markings, and you feel they belong on the mantelpiece rather than in the saucepan. But they're truly delicious to eat, the whites translucent with freshness and the yolks slightly flavoured with crab. Any guilt we may have felt was diminished by the thought that herring gulls, which look so noble over the sea, can be nasty predators, cruising up and down the beach looking for the eggs and chicks of the plovers.

The island was also home to a colony of black guillemot and to a fair number of eider duck. Both these species have almost disappeared since the advent of the mink. We miss the brilliant black and white plumage of the drake eider, and his delicious wooing noises in the spring; no wonder the female always looks so contented and demure. The black guillemot was also a favourite, with its flight low over the water, red legs scuttering, and its devotion to its chick, often carried on its back. Mink are good swimmers, and one summer one managed to reach the grey islands, a mile out in the middle of the Sound, and wiped out a whole generation of tern chicks. That colony of common terns was once reputed to be the biggest in Britain, but since the deadly visitations began it has only just managed to survive. I've tried to catch mink in a mammal trap by the shore at Inninmore but so far not succeeded. Apart from a dead one on the island, I've never actually seen mink in the bay, and I've wondered if they're deterred by the otters, which are never far away.

In summer a pair of mute swans usually comes and nests on the island. On calm days they sometimes swim over to our beach, their elegance somehow out of place in those wild surroundings. One of a previous pair had a foot missing, perhaps through entanglement with a fishing line, but on the water the bird still looked effortlessly serene. Recently, not far from their nest on the island, we found a dead mink lying beside a sucked out swan's egg. This conjured up pictures of a desperate fight, unwitnessed in the wilderness. Did the swan stand and defend its nest against the all-conquering predator? Did it somehow manage to seize the animal in its beak and immobilise the jaws before they could be sunk into that long and vulnerable neck? Did it hold the struggling mink under water in the nearby pool until it drowned? If only David Attenborough had been there to record it.

The divers, all three of which may be seen at Inninmore, are true aristocrats of the sea. Great northern divers appear individually at any time of year; we presume they're immature birds taking their gap year before they settle down to breed. Red-throated divers come each spring. We're first aware of them when we hear a cackling call from high overhead and look up to see two tiny silhouettes shaped like backward crucifixes heading out to the Sound. They spiral down and land a mile or more out to sea, but their mournful wail carries to the land on a still evening, if the gulls will only be quiet for a moment. This pair nests on an island in a lochan that lies in a hollow of the hills to the north-east, where they can feed their chick either on the local brown trout or on sand eels from the Sound. Black-throated divers also appear from time to time. At a distance it's not always easy to distinguish between divers and shags when they're on the water, nor between the three species of diver. We're noticed that shags push up a little out of the water at the outset of their dive, making it look clumsier than the effortless submergence of the divers. Another way shags can be distinguished is their habit of congregating in excited parties of up to twenty or more (my cousin Wynn assures me that the collective noun for a group like this is "an orgy of shags"). The great northern divers we see are always solitary and look bulkier than their cousins, and when they're close enough you can make out the beginnings of the chequered black and white markings that resemble a policeman's cap band. The books say that the red-throated diver can be distinguished from the black-throated by the more upward tilt of its bill, but they haven't yet obliged me by sitting side by side in profile long enough to allow the comparison.

Even common garden birds somehow seem more exotic in the Western Highlands. In winter a flock of chaffinches comes to feed on the crumbs from the washing up water that's chucked onto the grass. The plumage of the males is much more vivid than that of their city counterparts, as if enlivened by the fresher air and a healthier life style. Even the black and white of the wagtails look more striking than elsewhere. When a visitor from suburbia made a nameplate to go over the front door, it was disregarded by the postman but much appreciated by a pair of wagtails, who built a nest behind it and entertained us by running around the front lawn chasing daddy longlegs. In winter twittering gangs of little birds, mainly tits but also a few tree creepers and goldcrests, episodically surround the cottage. On one occasion I managed to include Britain's smallest and largest (at that time) birds in the same field of vision, a goldcrest exploring a gorse bush with a golden eagle soaring in the background. Not so obviously exciting are the meadow and rock pipits that abound along the shore and pipe their objection to your trespass. An American visitor, at the time of President Johnson, used to refer to them all dismissively as LBJs (little brown jobs), but a more discerning friend points out that meadow pipits can be readily distinguished from rock pipits, not by the colour of their legs, as the books advise, but by whether they alight in the grass or on a stone.

Meadow pipits are the main targets for the cuckoos that come each spring. After many hours of watching cuckoos moving round the hillside, I hit upon a possible an explanation for their conspicuous and somewhat hawk-like appearance and their ridiculously obvious call. These characteristics are both the opposite of what you might expect in a predator that relies on stealth. However they could serve the purpose of helping them discover the whereabouts of the nests of small birds, which can't fail to notice the predator and fly out to scold it. Meadow pipits' nests are very well concealed, and even a sharp-eyed cuckoo must need to employ special tactics to find them. When I'd been watching a pair of cuckoos flying separately and apparently at random around the same patch of hillside, the idea struck me that perhaps the male was luring the owners of a nest away so that the female could sneak in and lay unnoticed. Sadly this theory, which I thought was rather ingenious, didn't last for long, being politely but firmly dismissed by the expert on cuckoos I consulted when I got home.

Flowers and plants

Inninmore is a treasure house for botanists, just as it is for geologists and ornithologists. Not being a botanist I can't attempt a comprehensive flora, but I hope I can convey something of the impression the plants and flowers make on people who go there. The character of the place depends as much on its vegetation as on its topography. The cycle of the year is reflected in the dominant colours of the plant world, which in turn provide a background for the diurnal rhythm of the light and for the unpredictable motifs of sun and cloud. These three themes – the tilt and the rotation of the earth and the perturbations of its envelope of air - combine in a symphony that determines the mood of the moment. In winter the bog and the upper slopes of the hill are bleached pale yellow by a million dead stems of reed and moor grass. In the spring bright greens appear, patchy at first then spreading like a rash to cover most of the land.

early August

With summer the stronger green of bracken emerges and soon dominates, interspersed with reddish-brown patches of sedge and bog asphodel on the slopes and the flush of bluebells in the meadow. In the autumn there's a sea change as the bracken fronds die back and turn to russet brown. This brown persists through the winter and on into the spring, light where it's dry and a rich dark when it's sodden, with a sharp demarcation between the two where sun and shadow meet. In autumn small patches of purple heather may appear at any level from shore to hilltop. The plant of all seasons is the gorse, with its furze a soft bluey-green and flowers a brilliant yellow on even the dullest day. In the winter the woods to the west show an infinite variety of overlapping little brown whorls, tinged in early spring with the purple of swelling buds. In the summer the browns are supplanted by an equal variety of greens, yielding in autumn to exotic flares of ochre and gold.

A prisoner in the cottage could follow the seasons from the succession of flowers that appear in make-shift vases on the table. In early spring come hazel catkins, their neat yellow pendants complemented by the upward arching tufts of last year's reeds. At Easter there are primroses galore, enough to fill a bathtub. A discerning florist may also have picked more reticent woodland flowers, such as dog mercury, wood sorrel, coltsfoot, tiny ferns and windflowers. But the most dramatic flowers of early spring, blackthorn, remain unpicked in their thickets of fierce spines, their frothy white looking as delicate as a Japanese painting against the backdrop of the cliffs. After another week the first violets and celandine appear on the table, and in May kingcups from the bog and bluebells from the meadow combine in a tin mug to epitomise the sun and sky of the Inninmore spring. In June there are foxgloves, flag iris and new reed heads, which look best all standing together in the aluminium water can. As you walk among the trees in the evening a waft of scent leads you to a rambling honeysuckle, which you can pull down and carry back, together with wild roses, to sweeten the bedroom. By high summer our prisoner will be able to identify a whole new array of delicate little flowers brought in from the meadow where the sheep have kept the turf short: sheeps-bit scabious, harebells and milkwort, all in varying shades of blue; pignut and eyebright, both feathery white; the purple and mauve of knapweed and thistles. Wild thyme adds further tiny flecks of purple and a miniature hypericum scatters little stars of gold, but the posy will be dominated by the yellow heads of buttercup and hawkweed. Hawkweed is a plant of particular significance at Ardtornish because John Raven, as a young amateur botanist, distinguished new sub-species by the different arrangements of the hairs on their stems and got them officially recognised in the British flora.

One flower our prisoner will never see displayed in a jar is grass of Parnassus, whose virginal purity defies such ravishing. This plant grows on the edge of the bog and is at its peak in mid-September. It's always scarce and some years you may not find it at all, but if you're lucky, among the constellations of yellow buttercups you'll catch sight of a single white flower on a leafless stem. Its five petals, veined with green, alternate with bright green stamens, and its perfect symmetry and erectness confer an aristocratic air. To a casual observer the bog looks impoverished and dull, but it's the setting for many little gems, grass of Parnassus the most lustrous pearl among them.

grass of parnassus

Or the plants can be described by where they grow, starting at the sea and working upwards. Along the shore, the curving lines of drying bladder wrack reflect the phases of the moon. The winter gales toss up a tangle of other vegetation from the sea, including holdfasts, the anchor roots of kelp, which normally only shows itself as a gently waving brown forest just below the surface at low tide, while the acid greens and delicate coral pinks of smaller seaweeds are also laid out for display along the sand. Above the shingle, in the transitional zone covered only by the highest tides, you'll find tiny salt-tolerant plants such as sea spurge, sea spurry, scurvy grass (did sailors once eat this?) and moonwort. A little higher up is a band of pink sea milkwort and thrift, trimmed on its upper margin with a delicate hem of tormentil and silver weed. Where the burn meets the beach to the south-west of the cottage it breaks up into a delta, forming bizarrely-shaped little islands each covered with a rich baize of low grasses. The children used to delight in leaping from one to another of what they called "the Chinese islands," braving a fall into the stinking black mud between them.

The bog, which starts just above the shore, holds a collection of curious plants, some spotted, some strikingly coloured and all vaguely threatening, such as butterwort, spearwort, lousewort and spotted orchid. None of these lasts when picked, even though they grow in waterlogged soil. Strangest of all is the sundew: little blobs of glue shine invitingly round its hinged plate-like flowers, and the larder of insects within attests to its deadliness. It's quite a relief to come across more ordinary plants such as meadow buttercup, spearmint and vetches. In summer the pink hues of ragged robin, willow herb and purple loosestrife stand out against the green of the reed beds and the white of meadowsweet.

The turf around the cottage and in the meadow, well grazed by sheep and deer, provides a habitat for many meadow flowers. A rare and special find is the field gentian, with its bell-shaped flowers of exquisite blue. Many of the favourites of childhood abound here: daisies, campion, clover, lady's smock, bacon and eggs, fox and cubs, eyebright, speedwell, herb robert, stitchwort and vetches. There are also plants less popular with children, such as goosegrass, burdock, thistles and stinging nettles, whose antidote, the dock, can usually be found not far away.

In the wood higher up are some of the best flowers of all, those of the trees. The hazel catkins, pussy willow, blackthorn and bird cherry shout out at you, but you have to look more carefully for the brown catkins of the birch and the green catkins of the alder, the little pale green shields of wych elm, the yellow tassles of the oak, and, later, the bursting yellow stars of the ivy, much-frequented by hover-flies and wasps.

Above the trees, where the hill steepens towards the crest, the thin coating of soil is often worn through to give rocky slopes, dry stream-beds and patches of scree. The plants have to be able to withstand the summer droughts and the gales and torrents of winter, so the vegetation is strong and wiry. On the slopes there are hummocks of heather, both bell heather, with its purple-crimson flowers, and the paler pink of ling. Cascading mats of wild thyme give another shade of purple, while even at this height harebells and tormentil add touches of a brighter hue. In spring there are violets in the more sheltered spots, and in summer there is clover. But where bracken hasn't invaded it's the grasses and sedges that prevail. We take these humble plants for granted, but if you look at them carefully you'll be astonished by their wonderful variety of flower-heads, some soft and feathery, some firm and spiky, some nodding, some erect, and varying in size from cocksfoot three feet tall to tiny creeping fescues. It's the sedges that give the hills their ginger and green tints in spring and autumn. In damp areas there are rushes and cotton grass, while on the tops there are never-ending clumps of tussock grass. In contrast, in the shelter of the little ravine where the main burn comes to the edge of the cliff we've found the delicate heads of water avens nodding over the chasm below, and once, in September, some perfect field mushrooms embedded in the turf.

Trees

The slopes to the west of Inninmore, where the path runs, were probably once covered in their entirety by native broadleaved woodland. This would account for the copious bluebells, originally flowers of woodland, that still flourish in the open patches. Woodland, particularly oak, was an important economic asset in the 18th century, and many oakwoods, for example those to the east of

Loch Sunart, were fenced off and managed by coppicing and pollarding. The bark was stripped off and used for tanning, while the timber was in demand for a variety of purposes, including boat-building, barrel-making and pit props. The Duke of Argyll, who then owned most of Morvern, considered fencing off the Inninmore woods but seems to have decided instead to exploit them for charcoal (see page 130). As a result the more accessible areas were gradually denuded of trees and only the steeper slopes remained untouched. Once charcoal burning ceased, the main threat to the woods came not from humans but from deer and sheep. However the fertility of the soil overlying the basalt and sandstone has allowed the trees to keep regenerating with sufficient vigour to keep pace with the constant browsing. More recently the estate has introduced a new policy by which sheep have been removed from this area entirely while deer numbers are more strictly controlled. It will be interesting to see the difference this makes to the wood. Already more saplings are growing up, and it's likely that the wood will become thicker and its margins will spread outwards more rapidly. The path will get more quickly overgrown, because there'll be fewer feet to keep it trodden down and fewer teeth to trim the sides. Perhaps also the tree canopy will eventually become denser and make it harder for plants to thrive beneath, with a consequent reduction in insects and birds.

The main native trees are oak, ash, birch, rowan, willow and wych elm. Some trunks are clad in ivy, and there are occasional hollies and bird cherries. The undergrowth is of hawthorn, hazel, blackthorn, wild rose and brambles. When you're going along the path your attention - and your clothing - is particularly caught by the brambles, which thrive in the semi-shade. The leaf mould beneath is perpetually moist and quickly turns to a friable loam, redolent of fertility and supporting a wide variety of flowering plants, ferns, mosses and fungi. Insects abound. The richness of the ecosystem has been recognised by the designation of the area as a Site of Special Scientific Interest.

The oaks are of the sessile variety, growing into a globular shape and not achieving the height of their parkland cousins. Indeed no tree can grow very tall here because the shallowness of the soil doesn't allow roots to go deep enough to make a firm anchorage against the gales. The ashes are quick to grow and quick to die, and the upper branches of older specimens tend to become skeletal. Thirty-five years ago Celly and I planted three ash saplings just to the south-west of the cottage door, partly to give shelter from the prevailing wind and partly to celebrate our three children, George, Laura and Alex. We had to put a shield of blackthorn and brambles around them to prevent the deer nibbling them to death, which would have been a terrible portent. Happily trees and children have all thrived wondrously.

Wych elms, like sessile oaks, are also more globular than the traditional slender elm of English parkland. Although they might not make it to the catwalk they're beautiful in form and colour, and those at Inninmore have so far managed to escape the disease that's killed or mutilated so many trees elsewhere. The wych elms around my home in Yorkshire, for example, have all lost their main stems, but defiantly keep sprouting round the base, many coming to assume a lowlier role as the component of a hedge. The deer particularly like the bark of wych elms, perhaps for medicinal purposes, or perhaps as a food of desperation at the end of winter. If too much bark is stripped off, the tree won't survive, but if it isn't ringed completely it may recover, with a scar that stays for life and may one day break down to form a home for a tawny owl. One such tree, self-sown and now about 25 years old, is growing just behind the cottage. It was soon attacked by the deer, so we protected it with a tangle of barbed wire. It's been left with a scar, lipped with raised edges, but as yet no hole and no owl.

Deer are also very partial to holly, despite its prickles, and holly is only likely to avoid mutilation if it's growing in an inaccessible place. Often the lower leaves keep getting nibbled off so that the tree grows into the standard shape that nurserymen grow for formal gardens. The same has happened to a hawthorn bush that chose to grow on our front lawn, though in this case I think the gardeners were sheep rather than deer. We wish the deer would eat more alder, which seeds itself along the sides of the burns. It grows up very rapidly and gets in the way when you're fetching water or having a wash. And it provides shelter for the midges. The deer nibble young alder enough to make it grow more densely but not enough to kill it. The final piece of woodland on the path before you get to the cottage is a grove of close-set alders, their stems grown tall and straight in their competition for the light. In contrast,

a single alder growing in the open can turn into a broad and handsome specimen. For many years one stood by the bridge over the burn to the east, forming a familiar feature of the landscape. On its lowest branch we made a swing from stout rope and an old motor tyre, both delivered by the tide to the beach nearby; George used it to launch himself over the burn yelling like Tarzan, while Laura preferred to sit in it rotating gently, first one way then the other, in the dreamy manner of little girls. The top branch of this tree once gave me a special treat when a lesser grey shrike, a very rare visitor, perched on it long enough for me to compare it with its picture in the book. Alders don't make old bones, and this one eventually died and bit by bit found its way to the log pile. To make up for its passing six years ago I planted some Scots pine saplings in the meadow just beyond, in a wire compound just above the shore like a miniature Guantanamo Bay. I got the saplings when they were just a few inches high from Maggie Kennedy's tree nursery at Durinemast, a cottage in another part of the estate of similar age and style to Inninmore. They've all grown vigorously and will soon have to be thinned out. I ask the guardians of the SSSI to appreciate what they add to the landscape and to let them stay as my memorial.

There are occasional bird cherries in the wood. In spring they declare themselves as puffs of white amid the general green, and in winter the blackness of their stems stands out against the browns of other trees. On more level ground they appear to grow in clumps, but when you get close you see that in fact it's just one tree with several branches radiating out and propped on the ground, like an octopus leaning on its elbows. The bird cherry that gave the waterfall its name has now been replaced by an even more exotic species, a cotoneaster. So far as I know cotoneasters aren't native in Morvern, so I can only suppose that this one was brought from a distant garden in the gut of a bird that came to feed on the cherry. Trees have some imaginative ways of spreading. Just above the eastern end of the beach at Inninmore is a small clump of aspens. Since there are no other aspens for miles around, the seed must have floated in by sea, been deposited at the high tide mark, then dried out and been blown up among the rocks above. Aspens send out lots of suckers, so that a single tree soon turns into a clump.

The gorse that fringes the shoreline is a mixed blessing. At a distance the bushes are an attractive shape and colour, and their brilliant yellow flowers are unfailingly there to cheer you up in the gloomiest months of the year. In spring their prickly depths attract stonechats and chaffinches to nest, and there's always a song thrush not far from the cottage. But they spread rapidly, and if unchecked they coalesce into a screen that blocks off the view and makes us feel hemmed in. Every few years we don leather gauntlets like Hardy's furze-cutter and cut them back to the roots. But it's a battle we can't win, like fighting the Hydra, because several new shoots soon sprout where the original was cut off. Unfortunately sheep and deer don't seem to like young gorse shoots, although they look succulent enough. A fortune awaits the geneticist who engineers a sheep that feeds on gorse, bracken and brambles. You have to wait a few months before the cut furze will burn; but once it's turned brown and dry it flares up eagerly and gives out copious black smoke, which once alarmed a helpful observer on Mull so much that he phoned the estate to say the cottage was on fire. The thicker stems we save for firewood. Gorse wood is dense, burning slowly and giving out a steady heat, ideal for making bread.

Sheep don't eat brambles but they sometimes make curious circular clearings in them, like crop circles, eight feet across. This happens when a sheep is reaching for something tasty at the edge of a bramble bush and gets its fleece caught on a strong shoot. Instead of sitting down and working out how to disentangle itself, as any sensible animal would, it rushes around in a circle trying to break the tether, trampling the bush right down and leaving little tufts of wool snagged around the edge. I'm told that sometimes a sheep caught like this may get irretrievably tangled up and starve to death, but fortunately all I've found are the signs of successful struggles.

The sequence of re-colonisation by trees at the edges of the wood is interesting. Alders are the pioneers, seeding themselves along the burns, followed by wind-borne birch and ash, and then bird-borne hawthorn and rowan. Where there are no sheep, hazel saplings spring up in open ground some distance from the nearest parent tree. Since there are no squirrels, we presume the nuts are carried by relays of mice, each pilfering in turn from its neighbour's larder and scampering away to deposit the nut a few yards further on. Oaks and hollies don't usually appear at the tree party till later.

The wood at the western end of the path near Inninbeg is quite different in character, having been planted some 200 years ago with non-indigenous species such as beech and exotic conifers. The planting was no doubt to improve the view from Ardtornish House, which was built in the mid-18th century on the headland just above Old Ardtornish Castle. Around the site of house and in the bay nearby are many mature horse chestnuts, limes and sycamores. The last must have been esteemed as stylish and aristocratic at the time they were planted, though today they're looked down on as common intruders. The trees outlived the house whose outlook they were intended to enhance. When Octavius Smith bought the estate of Ardtornish to add to the estate of Achranich in 1859, he became the owner of a second fine mansion house. When Octavius died in 1871, his son Valentine inherited all his property and became a very wealthy man. Despite the attractive but unadorned appearance of Ardtornish House, captured on photographs taken by his sister Gertrude, and despite its magnificent situation overlooking the Sound of Mull, and despite the pleasure it had given to the family and to numerous visitors, Valentine allowed it to become derelict. He seems to have done this mainly to reduce his expenses, for much the same happened when he acquired Lochaline House a few years later. Ardtornish House was finally demolished in 1907 by Gertrude, who had inherited the estate on her brother's death the previous year and was dismayed to find the house she had loved in such a bad condition. Today many of the trees planted to embellish the view have outgrown their roots and are succumbing to the gales, as if having lost the will to live without the house from which they were so long admired. Most of them won't be capable of natural regeneration, and in time the slopes once planted with exotic specimens will revert to bracken and native woodland.

Small creatures

The only unwelcome creatures at Inninmore are little ones: mice, midges, sheep ticks and horse flies. Mice may look sweet as they sit on a packet of biscuits and clean their whiskers, but they do a lot of damage and make quite a mess. They were there long before us and, although we may have temporarily reduced their numbers, we've never been able to evict them completely. They multiply even faster than rabbits, and particularly like to make their nests in stored clothes or bedding. What cosier place to rear a family than a well-chewed ball of the finest wool in the depths of an Arran sweater? We soon learnt that the only way to protect clothes was to take them away with us, and to protect bedding was to hang it on a line. Someone omitted to do this with a beautiful patchwork quilt that Heather had been painstakingly stitching for over a year: within a fortnight it was irretrievably ruined. Mice easily chew their way into plastic containers, and often we arrive to find our stores of porridge and pasta have been liberally sprinkled with dark specks that look like coarse pepper. Then there's the dilemma of whether you just scrape off the top layer, don't tell anyone and risk the dreaded *Salmonella typhimurium*, or throw the whole lot away and go short till the next shopping expedition. Mice also seem to enjoy chewing plastic and rubber just for fun; they've made holes to empty several fuel containers and damaged two inflatable dinghies beyond repair. Their scuttling keeps you awake at night: it's not the volume of the noise but its unpredictability, and the anxiety about what's going to be chewed next.

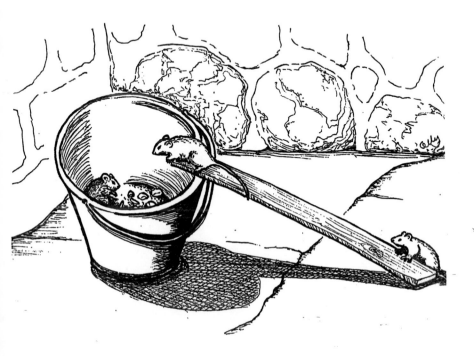

We've shied away from using poison, partly because of Aunt Emmeline and partly because we thought there'd be putrefying corpses everywhere. We've tried most types of mousetrap, and none of the expensive modern ones performs any better than the traditional Little Nipper. When the children were small, once they'd seen a dead mouse in the trap with its body stiff and eyes bulging, they forbad me to use them any more Instead we devised a humane trap by putting a ramp up the side of a plastic bucket with cheese in the bottom: the mouse would run up the ramp and jump down into the bucket, but when it had eaten the cheese it wouldn't be able to climb back up the shiny sides. We caught several in this way and took them down the beach to release them. They probably all soon found their way back for a second helping. But the mood changed after the mice had chewed a hole in the tummy of the teddy bear: no death was then too cruel. I put out several traps and gathered two harvests every day, one before I went to bed, the other first thing in the morning. I sometimes caught a dozen or more in a single night, but still they came. They evidently take the understandable view that it's their home more than ours. They must see us as huge and unpredictable intruders who bring vast quantities of food but greedily consume most of it and hide the rest away in tins. When, occasionally, we do leave them a choice morsel, it may prove to be the prelude to a violent death. Catching them gives me mixed feelings, as I tried to express in this little poem in the visitors' book:

O mouse,
You left your calling cards
On the table and on the shelf
And in the porridge jar,
Most sociable mouse.

I returned your call
With my wooden card
Embossed with wire
And scented with cheese.

Now at last we meet
Face to face,
You, staring pop-eyed in surprise,
Me, rather regretful.

If you ask any summer visitor what they most dislike about the Highlands they'll groan and say "the midges". The midges of Morvern are particularly famed for their numbers and ferocity, and are alleged to keep many tourists away. But it's hard, as they assail you, to be grateful for their part in the preservation of the wilderness you're enjoying. Midges flourish along the west coast of the Highlands in the same months as do mackerel, namely May to September. Their normal food is the sap of grasses, but the females need a sip of mammal blood to make them fertile. They attack only in certain weather conditions, particularly in the early morning and evening when the air is still and humid, though sometimes they may surprise you by appearing in the middle of the day. First there's a single scout, which gives out pheromones of delight when it finds you. Then a circling horde appears from nowhere, like myriads of tiny vultures. Then they all start zooming in for the attack, piercing you with needles around your eyes, in your hair, on your ears, neck, ankles, wrists and other parts you'd never have thought they could get at. On the first encounter their bites produce just little red marks and brief irritation, but once you've become sensitised you tend to develop lumpy spots that tickle for days. It's hard to resist scratching them, especially if you're four years old, and sometimes they get infected and sore.

A brisk wind or hot dry sunlight will banish midges, at least for the time being. I've tried all sorts of other measures – head nets, ointments and potions, running down the beach, rowing out to sea – but I've found only one that I can recommend. Although one or two stragglers may stick in your hair, midges don't follow you indoors *en masse*, so whisky drunk in a back room will invariably bring relief. One rugby-playing friend, who prided himself on his toughness, scoffed when I warned him about the midges as he set off to Inninmore in a wet July. He returned much earlier than planned, a wiser and a spottier man. I've often wondered how the locals cope: perhaps constant inoculation from an early age confers immunity, or maybe, since reluctance to disrobe confers a reproductive disadvantage, natural selection over the millennia has led to the survival only of those impervious to midges.

Horse flies, or clegs as they're known locally, have a nastier bite but aren't nearly so numerous. Their flight is clumsy and their attacks are slow, so that you can often see them coming and slap them dead while they're making up their minds where to bite. They don't always attack bare skin, but sometimes land on clothes too thick for them to penetrate; perhaps, being used to piercing the hides of deer, they think they can stick their proboscis through anything. In contrast to the midges, horse flies are at their worst when the sun is hot, so you're most susceptible when you're sitting outside reading a book, especially if the story's coming to a climax and you're totally engrossed.

The tactics of sheep ticks are altogether different. They cling onto the fronds of bracken and other low herbage, waiting for an animal to brush past so that they can transfer for a meal. They must have extraordinary patience, because they're lurking everywhere and in most places animals don't pass very often. They go through several stages in their life cycle, and seem to like the blood of mammals at every one of them. When unfed they range in size from a tiny speck to a large pin head, though they swell to plump and purple peas if allowed to gorge. This is most likely to happen on a dog that has long hair or won't allow you to groom it. Their usual line of attack in humans is from the feet. They first get onto your socks, then climb up your trousers, preferably on the inside, until they reach somewhere warm enough to have a good blood flow and tender enough for their proboscis to penetrate. It's a wise precaution, after walking through bracken, to search the most likely regions before the ticks take hold. Once they've got stuck in they're very difficult to remove in one piece. Some people swear by a dab of iodine or paraffin, but neither works for me. Others recommend the touch of a lighted cigarette, which I've never dared to try. Usually I end up pulling the body off and leaving the head embedded. This still causes an itchy spot, but at least you don't get a purple pea. Like grooming in monkeys, a mutual search for ticks, carried out nightly by candlelight, can help you get more intimately acquainted.

But on one occasion ticks brought a tragic end to a promising romance. Two young people from the city had gone to the cottage on a sort of prenuptial honeymoon. They lay in the sun, went for walks, and lay in the sun again until supper and an early bed. After a few days both she and he found ticks on the more intimate parts of their bodies. Neither knew much about Highland entomology, but both of them, being well-informed and broad-minded, had read leaflets about venereal infections. Each was convinced that the other had infected them with pubic lice. They left next day in acrimony and never spoke to each other again. Another couple, both doctors who should have known better, were also put out by their misidentification of the ticks. After a few days at the cottage they were dismayed to find they were both infested. They were particularly concerned that they'd introduced the pests themselves and might have started an infestation in the bedding. Being responsible people, they took the trouble to go all the way to the nearest chemist, in Fort William, to buy an insecticide powder that would eliminate it. However, despite their best endeavours they didn't succeed in ridding Morvern of its ticks. Fortunately their marriage was strong enough to survive this little misunderstanding. To end the paragraph on a more cheerful note, I should add that there're also been a number of happy honeymoons at the cottage, and I dare say a number of happy conceptions on that beguiling brass bed.

violet ground
beetle

Apart from that one sad episode ticks don't seem to have done us any lasting harm. So far no one has contracted Lyme disease, but I always worry when one of us has a strange rash. Not all little creatures at Inninmore are nasty. There are many lovely butterflies and moths, some of them quite rare, and handsome beetles go scuttling about their business through the grass. In late summer large dragon flies, mottled blue and black, hover majestically then zig-zag off at lightning speed in low-level combat. For years a colony of slow worms has lived in the stones and slates beside the byre. From about April one or two may glide out to see if it's warm enough for sun-bathing, moving just a few inches at a time until it gets hotter. The children at first tried to pick them up, but desisted when their tails kept coming off. Our city couple said we should have warned them about the adders. Although most people say Morvern's climate isn't right for adders, I always scan the ground ahead when barefoot or in sandals. In the spring infanticidal frogs lay their spawn in little pools that often dry out before the tadpoles can mature. And on the hill in high summer you may get a glimpse of a lizard scuttling off to hide behind a rock.

Rabbits

There were rabbits at Inninmore until shortly before we first went there but they were eliminated by successive plagues of myxomatosis. A small colony lingered on at Old Ardtornish until the 1980s, and not long ago they were still plentiful on the slopes of Bheinn Iadain, a hill some eight miles to the north. An Australian zoologist has calculated the rate of spread of rabbits by observing the mean number of hops taken by young animals prior to first copulation. According to his formula, assuming they weren't once again cut down by myxomatosis, it would take them just over 23 years to spread from Bheinn Iadain back to Inninmore. In the late 1960s John Buxton, a naturalist who lives at Horsey in Norfolk but knows Morvern well, put some wild rabbits brought from Norfolk on Inninmore Island. His main purpose was to provide prey for the eagles, but he hoped that in addition puffins might be encouraged to come and nest in the burrows. Although John brought only two adults, they soon bred as only rabbits can, and a thriving colony developed. (Why, I wonder, don't rabbits pay a terrible price in deformities when they procreate in a fashion totally forbidden by canon law?). Sadly the puffins didn't take the hint, but the eagles enjoyed having an alternative supply of meat when gull chicks were out of season. On the island these rabbits were, literally, isolated from the disease, which never got across the water to infect them. But after more than 30 years free of predators except from the sky, they all succumbed to an even more deadly predator that came by sea, namely mink.

There were several reasons why we wanted to see rabbits back at Inninmore. They would add to the diversity of the wild life, without competing with other species. They would keep the grass down, which would encourage the growth of the little flowers that grow in the machair of the Hebrides – and would make our lawn look neater. The shelduck that visit the bay might stay to nest in their burrows, and the puffins that had spurned the island might, just possibly, prefer the higher cliffs on the mainland. They would be food for the eagles and for the foxes, reducing the number of lambs they took in the spring. They would be food for the buzzards further down the coast. They would also be a source of fresh meat for *homo sapiens* stranded far from his usual food supply, and would allow me to practise the rabbit-catching skills I'd learnt as a boy. And baby rabbits playing among the gorse bushes would look delightful.

The main problem about reintroducing them was of transporting genuinely wild rabbits there in a good enough state and in sufficient numbers to establish a breeding colony. Our first attempt was while we were living in Newcastle. The week before we were due to go to Morvern we put an advertisement in the local paper offering a pound each for up to ten live wild rabbits. A Geordie voice, who wouldn't give his name, phoned to say he'd bring us the rabbits the following evening, when we'd planned to set off, driving overnight when the roads were clearer and the children less fractious. We waited well beyond the time we'd wanted to leave but no one came. Finally, at 11 pm, just as we'd decided to give up and go, an old van drew up and a man came to the door carrying two lumpy moving sacks. He handed them over, took his money and left into the darkness. We transferred the contents to a box. There were ten rabbits, obviously very scared. They scuffled in the corners of the box and paid no attention to the lettuce and carrots we put beside them. On the advice of a vet friend, we gave five of the rabbits an intramuscular injection of 30 millegrams of phenobarbitone as a sedative, but it didn't make any obvious difference. We loaded the box in the back of the camper van between three sleeping children and set off. Early in the morning the protests of waking children rose to a crescendo and we stopped for a break. There was no sign of life from the box, and we couldn't resist checking to see that the rabbits were still alive. We opened the box cautiously and peeped inside: two rabbits shot out and sped away into the bushes. Then there were eight. We completed the journey without further peeps, though we wondered how the remaining rabbits were coping with the jolts as we bumped along the final stretch of pot-holed track to the beach, and whether they felt seasick as the boat lurched and tossed down to Inninmore. The whole journey took nearly 14 hours, and when we at last opened the box to let the rabbits go among the gorse bushes, at first they were too numb and dazed to run away. Then one by one they gathered their wits enough to hop clumsily away and disappear into the furze and sedge. I hoped they'd find protection in the nearby rock-fall until they were able to dig proper burrows. If they stayed in the open they'd be easy prey for the foxes and eagles. When I returned to the spot next morning I found two corpses, without obvious injury, lying stiff among the bushes. Then there were six. Next day there was another corpse, down on the beach. We never saw the remaining five, dead or alive, and when we returned in the autumn there were no droppings and no burrows anywhere. Our vet friend advised us that when wild rabbits are subjected to severe and sustained stress the shock causes adrenal haemorrhage, which kills them within 48 hours. We thought that these rabbits had probably been caught by snaring, which would have inflicted extreme stress even before they'd started their very stressful journey.

Some years later we made another attempt, this time with semi-tame rabbits that could be caught and transported with less stress. A friend with a small-holding reared some baby wild rabbits he'd found in a nest and crossed them with a domestic variety, with the hope of combining docility with ability to survive in the wild - traits that are probably incompatible. He gave us six friendly young creatures that looked like wild rabbits but didn't mind being handled. They were also not afraid of dogs, having grown up in the company of two sweet-natured Labradors. They seemed quite happy on the journey and joined us in a snack at our stopping points. Once at Inninmore we let them out in the same patch of gorse about a quarter of a mile away from the cottage, and watched them as they fed on the grass and lolloped about in the sun. Next morning they'd all managed to find their way to the front lawn, and though we kept removing them to various attractive homes around the bay, they kept on returning. On one occasion we saw Ranald's boat approaching. He was certain to disapprove so we tried to scare the rabbits away. We felt rather ludicrous waving our arms and saying shoo, but we managed to get them all out of sight before he landed. As we all sat on the bench outside the front door drinking coffee, out of the corner of my eye I saw a rabbit hopping back towards us. Hurriedly we drew Ranald's attention to some unsatisfactory feature in the other direction. He didn't see the rabbit and departed unaware of their presence. It was clear that their lack of wariness would make them easy prey for foxes, and that if anyone came with a dog they'd probably run up to greet it. When we left we wished them an optimistic *au revoir*, but we never saw them again.

Our third attempt failed for completely different reasons. This time we went for entirely wild rabbits again, but arranged for them to be caught in cage traps, not nearly as traumatic as snares, at Luke Gaskell's farm in the Scottish Borders, from where the journey would be much shorter. Luke's family were for a long time our neighbours in Morvern, being tenants of the cottage above Old Ardtornish Point. Luke's father Pip wrote a brilliant study, entitled *Morvern Transformed,* of the social changes that took place in the area in the 19th century, and various members of the family often came to visit Inninmore in their distinctive green dinghy of Scandinavian design. We'd already been staying at the cottage for a few days. The plan was that Luke's gamekeeper friend should trap the rabbits one evening while we drove back to the Borders to pick them up. We first had to take the white boat to Inninbeg, and in passing we paused to talk with Sarah Raven, John and Faith's daughter, who tenanted the large cottage in the bay with her husband Adam Nicolson. We'd thought it best not to seek the estate's formal permission to reintroduce rabbits because they'd feel obliged to say no, but we knew from previous discussions that most people thought it would be a good idea. We shared our intentions with Sarah, saying we'd be sailing back the next morning with a boatload of rabbits, and having sworn her to secrecy we set off for the Borders. All went according to plan. We arrived at Luke's farm to find two wooden boxes each containing six wild rabbits in prime condition, and after a pleasant evening and an early bed we drove back to Morvern next morning. We loaded the boxes onto the boat and set off back to Inninmore. We were just congratulating ourselves on the success of the exploit when we saw a launch bearing down on us at speed, like a customs cutter intercepting smugglers. As it got closer we recognised Faith in the bows. "You're not bringing rabbits, are you?" she shouted across at us. "Yes we are, actually. We thought they'd be a good addition to the wild life." "They'll eat all the trees," responded Faith; "look what happened in Australia." "There always used to be rabbits at Inninmore, and there are plenty of trees," I yelled. We were haranguing each other like rival coaches at the boat race. "But it's an SSI now," came the reply, "and it's against the law." Both sides now realised that a debate at high decibels over a cable's distance wasn't the best way to settle a complex ecological issue, and having made our points we both withdrew. After all the planning and effort that had gone into getting the rabbits safely there, we were in no mood to give them up lightly. We went ahead with landing the boxes on the shore and releasing the rabbits into the gorse. They briefly darted this way and that, then ran off and disappeared, apparently none the worse for the journey.

As I sat by the fire that evening quieter counsels prevailed. Having heard Faith speak quite favourably of rabbits in the past, I couldn't understand why she was now so vehemently against them. I didn't want to repay her kindness over the years with rank defiance. And when all was said and done, she was the landlord and I was the tenant. It was now the age of the mobile, and a telephone mast had recently been erected on the hill opposite us in Mull, so we were able to discuss the issue with more calmness and objectivity by phone. Faith told me that the estate had just received the first part of a large EU grant, totalling hundreds of thousands of pounds, to erect a fence that would keep sheep and deer out of the part of the estate that bounded Loch Linnhe, and so allow the natural woodland to regenerate. We'd seen the materials for the fence lying in piles on the hill, where they'd been delivered by helicopter, and had wondered what they were for. The second half of the EU grant would only be paid if the scheme was a success and in five years time there were lots of new trees growing where there had been few or none before. Faith was worried that our rabbits might multiply in Australian mode and eat all the lucrative saplings. Whatever my thoughts about use of EU money, I had no option but to promise to get rid of them. The rest of the family were appalled, but they knew that if I were forced to choose between the tenancy and them, they might well come second. I arranged to collect a shotgun and cartridges from Angus the next day, and when no one was watching I walked down to where we'd let the rabbits go. Several of them were out feeding or sunning themselves. They looked in good shape but hadn't yet learnt their way around, and it was quite easy to get close enough to shoot three of them. Heather, hearing the bangs, came running up in tears and said she'd divorce me if I shot any more. So when I gave Angus back his gun I told him I hadn't got rid of all of the rabbits but I'd shot as many as I could - which, in a sense, was true.

The villain of the piece (or the hero, depending on whether you're on the side of the saplings or the rabbits) was Adam Nicolson. To this day I'm not sure whether he passed the secret Sarah had shared with him on to Faith because of conjugal misunderstanding, loyalty to his mother-in-law, concern for the environment, anxiety about the estate's finances, or sheer mischievousness. Anyone who knows Adam will suspect it was at least partly the last. He expressed his contrition two days later when he walked down to Inninmore and was made to eat rabbit stew for supper. We couldn't quite bring ourselves to go and see how the surviving rabbits were faring in their gorse patch. Next time we visited there was no sign of them. I still hope that rabbits will flourish at Inninmore again one day, but I've promised Faith it won't be me who takes them there.

Larger animals

Apart from foxes all the larger animals are relatively benign. The foxes are very wild, and we smell them more often than we see them. The shepherds complain about the lambs they take, and in the winter they organise foxhunts along the wooded hillside to the west. The hounds work their way through the rocks and undergrowth, while a line of men with shotguns waits at the far end. But some foxes will always survive because the deep clefts and rock falls make impenetrable sanctuaries. During one of our visits a half-grown fox cub used to come each evening and feed from the dog's bowl on the lawn. We could easily watch it through the window in the lamplight. One of its legs was damaged, and we supposed that reduced ability to hunt had made it less cautious. There must also be badgers somewhere on the hillside, because we once found a dead badger cub curled up under the bench by the front door of the cottage. One evening a wildcat kitten (or what looked like a wildcat – I'm told that they're hard to distinguish from domestic cats gone wild) appeared outside the window and fed for a while from the dog's bowl, and adult cats have been seen sitting on the roof and even venturing into the cottage. If only we could train them to catch the mice. Two visitors have reported seeing a pine marten in the woods not far away, but I've never seen one myself.

There are large numbers of red deer on the tops. You'll nearly always see some when you go up the hill behind the cottage, and for many years Inninmore has been a favourite starting point for stalkers. I've never been stalking, but from what I've read it seems to combine the atavistic blood lust of the hunt with the quaint civilities of a privileged caste. First you have to be properly dressed, in tweeds, plus-fours and deerstalker hat. The person who is to fire the shot is called "the rifle," though the rifle itself may be carried for him by a ghillie until the moment comes to shoot. During the stalk you must follow the correct protocols, putting yourself under the direction of the stalker, a man who might at other times expect to take directions from you. He decides where you go, inspects beasts at a distance through a telescope, selects the victim and determines the approach, often leading you through several hours of effort and discomfort. You're not allowed to shoot until the stalker decides the time is right, which will be when you have a clear view of the chosen animal from less than 200 yards. The rifle is handed to you, you take aim and fire. If the beast falls there are murmurs of "Good shot sir," but a strained silence if you miss, or worse, if you hit but fail to kill. After you've briefly admired your trophy, you leave the body to be gutted and carried down the hill by

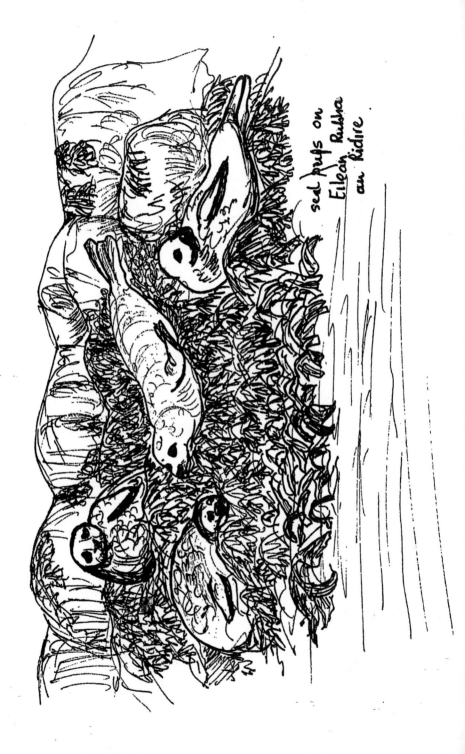

seal pups on
Eilean Rubha
an Ridire.

another ghillie. Apart from the final marksmanship, which isn't normally too difficult, success depends entirely on the field craft of the stalker, but the man who pulls the trigger claims the glory. A century ago deer stalking was of the greatest importance to the owners of Scottish estates. Until the 1920s the deer at Inninmore were fed throughout the winter on beans brought in by boat, and 20 years later Chubby Ives was still able to count over 400 stags on the eastern part of the estate where he worked. Today many of the estates make a good income by letting out their stalking to sportsmen from overseas, but the whole procedure is now more businesslike and the old rituals of the Highlands may be dying out.

In winter the deer come down to feed in the woods, where you more often hear them than see them, as they crash away dislodging cascades of stones. Sometimes your nose may lead you to a carcase, and quite often you'll come across shed antlers. People keep leaving antlers in the cottage as a thoughtful parting gift; if we'd kept the accumulation of 45 years we wouldn't be able to get in the front door. In the summer you mainly see the deer in the evening when they appear silhouetted on the skyline like Iroquoi scouts. They come down to the beach at night to eat the seaweed, and if you go out and shine a powerful torch you can see pairs of little round lights gleaming back at you. Or you may be woken in the early hours by the sound of snorting and munching as they browse the grass outside the bedroom window. But the noise made by a rutting stag on an autumn evening seems to come from a much more fearsome animal. You have to warn the children in advance or they'll think a monster is coming to get them, and as the weird and soulful groaning echoes round the hills even grown-ups can imagine a great hound bounding through the mist. Recently an unusually tame hind and her calf have been visiting the front lawn. She allows you to go up to within a few feet of her, and if you're patient and don't move abruptly she may even take food from your hand. We wonder if she was hand-reared elsewhere, and we fear for her fate when poachers next visit.

There are as many mammals in the water as on the land, the most plentiful being the grey seals that can nearly always be seen resting on the little rocky islets that lie just inshore of the main island. They come in all sizes, from plump sleek grandpas almost as big as a cow to pups the size of a spaniel. When you approach in a boat they lift their heads and look at you, then wiggle their hips (or where their hips would be if they had any), slide down into the water and disappear. A few seconds later dark round heads pop up all around and stare at you with bulging rheumy eyes, so that you feel that it's not they but you who's being observed and any moment a grandpa with a camera will emerge to film you. They're very inquisitive, and often come up beside you when you're out in a boat or a canoe. They seem to like it if we sing hymns to them, their favourites being *All things bright and beautiful* and *Abide with me.* They don't seem to like more military tunes such as *Onward Christian soldiers.* When the sea trout are running the seals come close inshore. When a seal ventures into the fish trap we drive it away by throwing stones, but usually it keeps coming back until we give up. We wonder how many fish it's catching in contrast to our own laborious and unproductive attempts. You can't count their catch because they consume it under water, but you never see a seal looking under-nourished. Seals appear to take life easy, spending most of the time resting on the rocks or floating just under the water with their noses pointing skywards, but then of course we never witness their amazing submarine agility. Occasionally, perhaps as part of courtship, they have bursts of gymnastic activity in which for ten minutes or so they repeatedly leap right out of the water, turn somersaults and perform hand-stands, as if they'd suddenly become aware of the need to do something about their weight.

You get used to the sight of seal heads in the bay, and it's easy not to notice that occasionally one of the dark dots is in fact an otter. There are otters all along this stretch of coast, where they have survived the general decline elsewhere, and you can often see one so long as you're quiet and patient and know where to look. Usually they appear in the evening close inshore as they dive for crabs and shellfish, sometimes munching them on the surface of the water, sometimes coming out onto a rock. If the birds resting on the promontory suddenly fly up, it's always worth looking through the binoculars for the lithe brown shape that's caused the alarm. Like the seals, the otters also come into the bay to catch sea trout. I've watched one less than 200 yards away in broad daylight, coming up onto the beach to eat its catch four times in half an hour, evidence of its amazing agility as well as its appetite. In calm weather you can sometimes make out an otter's head half a mile or more out; you can tell it from a seal by its more linear and purposeful passage and by a glimpse of an undulating body and tail behind the head. However on occasions otters can be surprisingly unwary, and I've seen one swim close to a yacht moored off the beach just as the noisy sailors were coming ashore in a dinghy to tell us, among other things, that it was a shame that otters now seemed to be extinct. We may see a female with two or three pups, or sometimes a solitary larger male. They must have a holt not far away, but we've never been able to locate it among the innumerable crevices and rock falls along the shore.

In fine summer weather we quite often see porpoises moving steadily down the Sound, their dark round backs looping up out of the water every 20 yards as they go. When it's very calm the first indication you get may be a snorting noise, the sound of their blowing travelling a mile or more over still water. They're probably there in rough weather too but we're not aware of them. On rare and special occasions we've had an encounter with a school of dolphins, which come and play around the boat with inquisitive delight. We've never seen a whale one in the Sound, although they're regular visitors elsewhere around the Hebrides.

Chapter Four: the past

Geology

[*Since writing this section, I've discovered that the Strontion granite begins at the mouth of Loch Linnhe, and that the rock at the end of our bay that we've always taken to be granite is in fact gneiss with copious granite within it.*]

Among the regular visitors to the cottage are geology students, and several have won doctorates from their observations there. I like to imagine them sitting at our driftwood table writing the first draft of their dissertations - though they must have found it difficult not to be distracted by the view. I've never managed to get to grips with geology, being put off by its unfamiliar terminology and unbelievable time scales. So the description that follows draws heavily on a leaflet written in 2000 by Professor J.R.Cann entitled *Geology of Ardtornish Estate,* a talk by Michael Brambell given to the Morvern Heritage Society in 2005, a scholarly entry in the visitors' book by Brendan Hamill, and observations by Paddy Hill, who has a special interest in the geology of this region. A proper exposition of the varied and complex geology of Morvern would take a volume in itself, so I'll confine myself to a brief layman's description of the features around Inninmore. These are of particular interest because of the unusual juxtaposition of the three main classes of rock, metamorphic, igneous and sedimentary. The burn that comes down the hill immediately behind the cottage marks the line of the Inninmore Fault. This is a major dislocation of the earth's crust at which the segment to the west has been displaced downwards by about 500 metres. The fault, which runs some way northwards, divides igneous and sedimentary rock to the west from much older metamorphic rock to the east.

The oldest of these rocks is the Moine gneiss, a hard metamorphic rock formed about 1,000 million years ago when sedimentary deposits that had been buried deep below the earth's surface were subjected to great pressures and temperatures. Moine gneiss forms the bedrock in most of the rest of Morvern, but at Inninmore it's found only for the first 100 yards or so to the east of the burn. It's black in colour, and the name "gneiss" means it tends to have a sheen. It has a banded texture and when the structure allows cleavage it may be called "schist" instead. I haven't been able to find out who or what Moine was. It has a rather coarse grain, and may contain veins of granite where the temperatures were high enough to melt the constituent materials. I discovered, the hard way, that gneiss as well as sandstone had been used to build the cottage, when I blunted two steel chisels while trying to hew out a larger space for the bedroom fireplace.

About 600 million years later, a mass of even harder rock pushed up from even deeper below the surface to form the high ground on the eastern side of Morvern, extending northwards to Strontian and at its south-western corner abutting the gneiss at Inninmore. This mass of rock, known as Strontian granite, evolved in a complex way from molten magma of variable chemical composition which crystallised into different colours, especially grey, pink and white, and into different patterns. As you walk eastwards down the beach, the first boulders you come to are of the dark gneiss, but further along are boulders with the lighter colours and smoother contours of the granite. At the end of the beach the sea has worn the base of the granite wall into huge round shapes, with comfortable recesses for bums of all sizes, where you can sit at ease and watch the sunset. We call this Henry Moore corner.

The beach nearby is made up entirely of multi-coloured pebbles, most of granite but some of gneiss, graded by the waves into sizes ranging from pigeons' eggs to rugby balls. It's hard to resist picking them up, and friends' houses throughout the land are embellished by paperweights and doorstops that were once washed by the tides at Inninmore. Strontian granite now goes much further afield and in far greater quantities from the huge quarry round the corner up Loch Linnhe, from which bulk carriers convey millions of tons across the oceans to make highways as far away as North America and Japan. And it is Strontian granite that now connects England to France in the lining of the Channel Tunnel. On the shore closer to the cottage there's a stretch of light-coloured sand, where the sand-eels burrow at the lowest summer tides, made up by particles of granite and seashells.

On the other side of the dividing burn can be found various types of sedimentary rock formed from deposits laid down following the downward displacement of the crust on the west of the Inninmore Fault. At the lower level, going right down to the shore, there are patches of sandstone, derived from the sedimentation of silica particles. The deposit nearest to the cottage contains a few thin seams of coal (see page 129), and is one of the most northern sites that coal has been found in the British Isles. The coal originates from about 300 million years ago when what is now Scotland was close to the equator and was covered by dense swamps of plants mainly of the horsetail type. Curiously, today's descendants of these plants, horsetails of a much smaller species, still grow on the surface above the coal seam, as if keeping vigil over the mass grave of their ancestors below. Not far away, in the stagnant water in the nearby bog, there are patches of iridescence on the surface, as on a puddle outside a garage, suggesting that there's oil somewhere about. Another sandstone deposit further west is most evident at a waterfall along the path, Bird Cherry Falls, where erosion of the comparatively soft stone has resulted in a high cascade with a hollow behind it. The rock here supports several different varieties of fern and makes an exotic place for a shower on a hot day. Further west still are the old sandstone quarries (see page 129). Half way up the hill are deposits of another type of sandstone, rich in calcium carbonate, known as cornstone; this can be recognised by the honeycomb of little hollow spheres eroded into it by rain. Higher up is a layer of limestone, derived from shells; similar deposits along Loch Aline used to be quarried and burned in kilns to produce lime. The limestone is rich in fossils, especially a type of prehistoric oyster *(Gryphea)* whose appearance has earned the nickname "devil's toenails." Fossils of various other types can also be found in the rocks at Inninmore. One visiting geologist kindly left a specimen of fossilised tree as a parting gift to the cottage, but I'm not sure exactly where he found it.

Four miles away, on the western side of the mouth of Loch Aline, is yet another type of sedimentary deposit, derived from the beach sand of the vast chalk sea that also gave rise to the white cliffs of Dover. This deposit consists of very pure silica that yields the high-quality glass needed for the manufacture of fine crystal and optical lenses. It has been mined continuously since the 1940s, so that the hill behind Lochaline is now honeycombed with tunnels. This is one of three instances in Morvern (the other two being the sandstone near Inninmore and the granite at Glensanda) where the quality of the rock and ready access by sea have given rise to a large commercial enterprise.

About 54 million years ago, in the upheavals accompanying Scotland's separation from Greenland, a huge volcano erupted in Mull. This volcano was centred on what is now Loch Ba and was about 30 miles across and over 20,000 feet high. Vast streams of lava flowed out in all directions to form dykes, which are vertical sheets where lava has tracked along fissures in the earth's crust. Dykes from this volcano even extended as far as the coast of Yorkshire, only 30 miles from my home. The lava cooled and solidified to form basalt, which caps many of the hills of Morvern, including those immediately to the west of Inninmore. This basalt is dark brown in colour and quite friable, so that masses have broken off the sides of the hills to form escarpments, such as the long escarpment that runs almost continuously above the path from Inninbeg. The ledges and crannies in the basalt cliffs make secure nesting places for eagles and ravens, while the topsoil that forms over the spoil below supports trees and plants better than does the granite to the east. Chunks of basalt continue to break off the escarpment from time to time, especially when it thaws after a period of hard frost, leaving scars of lighter brown along the cliff and partly covering up the sandstone deposits lower down. All along the shore here, and for some distance out to sea, there are massive boulders of basalt that have come bounding down the hillside. Polyphemus lives up there in the cliffs and hurls rocks at those who try to steal his sheep. In some places lava was forced up to the surface through cracks to form a swarm of dykes - which in other contexts might sound rather alarming. The basalt at Inninmore is unusually coarse-grained and sufficiently distinctive to have earned itself the name "Inninmorite."

The basic contours of the mountains and valleys of Morvern, like those of the rest of Scotland, result mainly from the collision of continents about 470 million years ago. In a cataclysm worthy of Tolkien, the ancient continent of Avalonia to the south collided with the continent of Laurentia to the north, the point of impact being not far from the present border between England and Scotland. The crust to the north gave way, buckling and folding like a concertina to create a series of mountain ranges with valleys and faults between them. One of these faults was then enlarged and deepened by the impact of another ancient continent, Baltica, which pushed the southern part of Scotland and England to the south-west. The resultant shearing force created the deep cleft in the earth's surface that we now know as the Great Glen, a section of which, Loch Linnhe, runs less than a mile away from Inninmore.

Over the aeons that followed, other forces, principally erosion, glaciation and volcanic eruption, modified the basic contours left by the continental collisions. Glaciation came on the scene quite recently by geological time scales, sculpting the shape of Morvern over the past two million years and conferring its name, which comes from the Gaelic *mor bhearna* (big valleys). The Sound of Mull was gouged out by a vast glacier, while Loch Aline was formed by a smaller glacier feeding into it. Two of the valleys you pass through when driving to Ardtornish, Glen Tarbert and the White Glen, are largely shaped by ice and contain many examples of moraines, the deposits left by the underside of a glacier. However the base of the White Glen has been largely filled up and levelled off by the deposits left by the river. The huge weight of ice once lying over the west coast pushed the whole crust downwards, but since the ice has melted the ground level has slowly risen again. In some places, perhaps including Inninmore (see page 132), this process has left raised beaches now fifteen feet or more above the high tide mark.

Archaeology and history

Most of the archaeological details in this chapter come from a survey of the Inninmore woods written in 2002 by Jennie Robertson, while most of the historical detail is taken from Philip Gaskell's book *Morvern Transformed* and from Iain Thornber's introduction to the 2002 edition of *Morvern, a Highland Parish* by Norman Macleod.

Inninmore has a number of features that favour human settlement: ready access from the sea, secure shelter for boats, flat ground that can be used for grazing cattle or growing crops, a good supply of wood, plenty of fish in the summer, and protection from northerly winds. Ready overland access to Morvern only became possible when roads were built at the end of the 19th century; prior to that the Sound of Mull was the major highway, with Inninmore a handy stopping point. People may well have lived there from pre-historic times, but no early artefacts have yet come to light.

The earliest evidence of human presence comes not from the remains of dwellings, which were originally built of materials

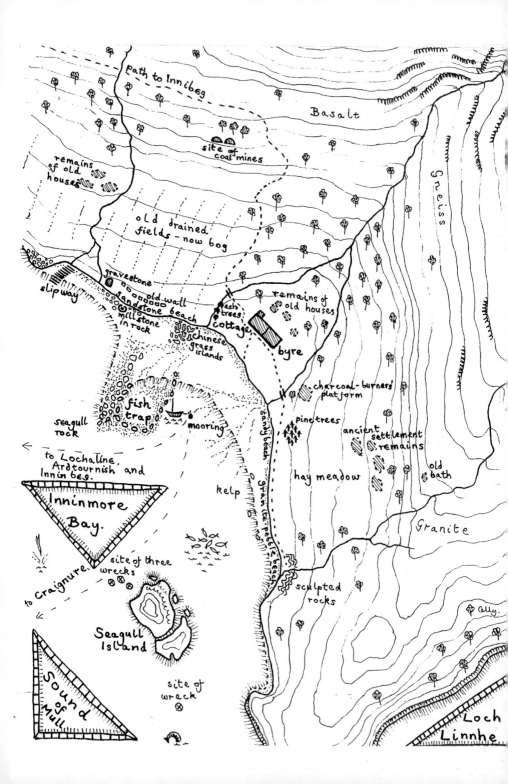

that didn't last, but from traces of economic activity. The earliest of these to be identified in the area is the sandstone quarry in the woods just above the shoreline about a mile to the west of the cottage. It's thought that this quarry was begun in the 12th century and continued in operation for about 700 years. The quality of the stone and its accessibility by sea made it in demand as a dressing in the construction of castles and churches for many miles up and down the coast, from Mingary Castle in Ardnurmurchan to Ardchattan Priory in Loch Awe. In the 19th century the stone was used in the construction of Eileen Musdile lighthouse off the western tip of Lismore and of the locks in the Crinan canal. It's an intriguing thought that such important and lasting structures should have taken their origins from amidst the transience and decay of the woods at Inninmore. The quarry stopped operating towards the end of the 19th century, and today its three worked rock faces can only just be made out through the overgrowth of trees, ivy, moss and ferns. Thirty years ago the remains of two quarriers' house could still be seen nearby, but these have now disappeared. On the shore just below are the remnants of a rudimentary jetty and several large blocks of sandstone, some with drill marks, still waiting for the next boat out.

An unexpected remnant of another human enterprise can be found just below the path some 400 yards to the west of the cottage. If you poke about among the bushes and bracken, you'll find two tunnels about four feet in diameter running horizontally into the hillside for a distance of 30 feet or so. Their roofs are dripping wet, their sides coated in ferns and their floors have pools of clear water. If you shine a torch, in the back of one of them you'll see the gleaming white bones of a deer that crept in to die or was dragged in by a fox many years ago. It's established that these tunnels were dug into the rock over 200 years ago to explore seams of coal that had been found in the surrounding sandstone. The seams proved too thin for exploitation, but the fact that they were discovered in so remote a spot, and that such arduous efforts were made to explore them, shows the value that coal must have had at the time the Industrial Revolution was taking off.

There are several groups of charcoal-burners' platforms along the more gentle slopes of the hill to the west, and a single platform is situated just beyond the burn to the east of the cottage.

Charcoal-burning was prevalent in the area in the late 18th and early 19th centuries, the product being sold for use in blast furnaces and possibly also for the manufacture of gunpowder. I wonder whether woodland may originally have covered all of the basalt slope to the west (see page 103), and whether the open patches that now interrupt it were cleared by charcoal-burners. A picture of Inninmore taken in 1919 by Robert Adam, a Scottish landscape photographer whose work can be viewed in the photographic archive of St Andrews University, shows that what is now mature woodland was then a sparser growth of younger trees. And even in the comparatively short time that we've been visiting, the margin of the wood has advanced 50 yards or so into the open areas. This suggests that the woodland has been steadily regenerating from an earlier clearance that may have been almost total.

Another mini-industry all around the coast of Morvern at about this time was the gathering and drying of kelp, which, when dried and burned, produced an alkali used for the bleaching of linen and in the manufacture of soap and glass. Kelp abounds in Inninmore Bay, at low tide emerging forlornly from out of the water like lost souls in Hades, but we haven't been able to identify any of the shallow pits in which it used to be burned.

The most recent attempt to establish an industry at Inninmore came in 1987, when Golden Sea Produce, a firm that operates numerous fish farms on the west coast of Scotland and is usually welcomed everywhere because of the benefits it brings to the local economy, applied to set up a salmon farm in the bay. There would be supporting buildings on the land, and electricity would be brought in by cable. It was an ideal site in some respects, being sheltered from the prevailing wind and scoured twice daily by strong tides. It seemed inevitable that the solitude would be spoiled forever. But when the official dealing with the proposal came to inspect the site he fell under its spell. "Unjustified intrusion into anchorages and areas of outstanding landscape," he wrote in his report, and, most unusually, rejected the application.

The most bizarre human relic can be found lying in the grass by the shore about quarter of a mile to the west of the cottage, in the form of two gravestones roughly hewn from the seam of sandstone nearby. The larger of these, measuring about five feet by three, is uninscribed. The other slab, two thirds the size, bears the crude inscription *"hear lays the remains of DMP."* The style of the lettering suggests that it was cut in the early 19th century. There are at least two theories about the identity of DMP: Jennie Robertson suggests the initials may be those of Donald McPhail, a shoemaker, whom the 1841 census records as living at Inninmore; while Chubby Ives thinks they may be those of Duncan Macpherson, a shepherd who lived there before the First World War. Whoever it was seems to have been obsessed with his own mortality, making his gravestone well in advance. When he died it must have been too heavy to be transported to wherever he was formally buried. We like to think that his soul prefers its solitary and unconsecrated memorial by the shore.

The sandstone deposit from which the gravestones were cut runs down to the sea. On its surface there are circular grooves, about four feet in diameter, plus smaller tool marks. This has been identified as a site from which millstones were cut. No millstones have been found at the Inninmore settlements, but one has been located on the bottom of the Sound some distance away, perhaps having toppled over the side of the boat while being transported in a choppy sea. If, in one brief moment of carelessness, the product of many hours' hard work was lost for ever, a few choice West Highland expletives may have rung out over the water.

The earliest human settlement mentioned in the literature is a group of dwellings in the wood half a mile to the west of the present cottage. All that now remains are vague outlines of small houses formed by moss-covered rocks on the hazel-covered slope. Pip Gaskell, from his researches and his own observations, suggests that there were five or six houses here. However he couldn't find them on maps drawn after 1755 and concluded that they were abandoned before this date. Jennie Robertson agrees that some of the outlines are of turf houses, but suggests that others may rather be of structures related to charcoal burning. On the shore just below this site the boulders seem to have been cleared away to make a slip-way where boats could be hauled above the tide line.

I've not been able to find any reference to the remains of another group of three or possibly five dwellings aligned along the base of the cliff at the edge of the meadow to the east of the cottage. These also consist only of rectangular outlines, measuring about 18 feet by 12, with a few low remnants of wall constructed from large unshaped stones, many too heavy for one man to carry. In some places the walls join up with the rock face behind them and in others they've been partly obliterated by rock falls. Scattered around them are lots of granite cobbles, of the same type as on the beach nearby. They may have been brought there to give drier and firmer footing where the ground gets boggy in the winter; alternatively they may denote the site of one of the raised beaches that can be found along the west coast (see page 128). A burn runs down from the hill nearby, and about 100 yards up its course there's a well-made rectangular stone trough that looks as though it was used for washing clothes. So far as I'm aware this particular settlement hasn't yet been the subject of formal archaeological study and its date hasn't been established.

There is broad agreement about the most recent settlement, which was situated close to the present cottage. Pip says that in 1770 five houses were occupied in this site, but by 1841 the number had fallen to two, and ten years later there was only one. The remains of three of the previous buildings are obvious. One has become the byre that abuts the present cottage: the walls are well preserved, and show the outline of a hearth on the western side, but the roof and possibly the cobbled floor are not original. The second is a much larger and newer-looking building about 50 feet behind the cottage. One gable end and other smaller bits of wall still stand, partly obscured by trees and bushes. The gable incorporates a chimney stack, but curiously this has neither hearth nor flue, as though it was just for show. The third building is much smaller and at some stage was partly converted into a shelter for animals, with corrugated iron sheets for a roof. The other two buildings can only be traced from outlines. There are several indications that the settlement here was once quite large and active. Most of the level ground on the flanks of the bay was drained and cleared of stones, to yield over an acre of good pasture to the east (now encroached upon by bracken) and a larger but wetter field to the west. Adam's 1919 photograph shows that the western field used to have an extensive drainage system, though now it has mainly reverted to bog. Hundreds of yards of stone wall were built, enclosing the western field and dividing the eastern meadow in half. A substantial fish trap was constructed, big enough to supply a small community. And on the beach there's an abundance of small shards of pottery of many different designs, mostly early Victorian.

There's no record that this settlement was deliberately cleared of people to make way for sheep, but the population seems to have dwindled at about the same time as large-scale sheep farming was being introduced and crofters were being evicted in other parts of Morvern. There's a risk of confusion with another settlement called Inninmore (more often known as Unnimore or Inniemore) situated near Loch Teachus, about ten miles to the north-west. This other Inninmore was cleared in 1824 with unusual heartlessness by Christina Stewart, a middle-aged maiden lady living in Edinburgh, who was the absentee proprietor of

Glenmorvern, an estate situated to the west of Lochaline. *Morvern, a Highland Parish* includes an account of these evictions, translated from the Gaelic, by "Mary of Unnimore," who was one of the victims. Mary's story quite rends the heart, and when it was published many years later provoked much anger against the perpetrators. In 1844 Patrick Sellar, infamous for the clearances he'd previously carried out in Sutherland, bought Ardtornish estate as it was then (now Old Ardtornish), which included the Inninmore that's the subject of this book. However three years previously the census had recorded only two households there, which suggests that the population had already fallen before Sellar arrived. Until the beginning of the 19th century the whole of Morvern belonged to the Dukes of Argyll. In 1819, however, the profligate 6th Duke had to sell off Morvern piecemeal to meet his gambling debts. Ardtornish was bought by the sitting tenant (or tacksman, as this type of tenant was termed), John Gregorson. Gregorson had a reputation for treating his sub-tenants well, but it's possible that he was obliged to reduce their number as a pre-condition of the sale to Sellar. During the 19th century a total of 3,250 people emigrated from Morvern, either voluntarily or because of eviction.

Friends sometimes comment on the discomforts we choose to put up with during our brief summer sojourns at Inninmore. But we live like kings compared with those who worked and lived there all the year round in earlier times. Some idea of what their lives must have been like can be gained from Isabel Grant's book *Highland Folk Ways* and from the folk museum she established at Kingussie. If you could transport yourself back two centuries, the first thing to strike you would be the lack of personal space. The dwellings were much smaller than the present cottage, many consisting of a single room, sometimes divided by a partition. Yet the families living in them were often large, with perhaps as many as eight children (not counting the two more who, on average, would have died in infancy), plus grandparents, all living under the same roof. There would be no privacy, and the whole household would have to endure at close quarters the loquacity, snoring, coughing and flatulence of each member. Glass was at a premium, so windows were small and often partly closed by shutters, and it wouldn't have been very light indoors even during the day. After dusk, which in mid-winter comes at 4.30 p.m., it would be very dark, with the glow of the fire supplemented by pools of light around the rush lamps. You'd have needed good eyesight to be able to read or to sew. What did they do on those long winter evenings? Story-tellers, musicians and singers would come into their own. Everybody would have gone to bed early, a form of partial hibernation that may account for the size of the families. The earlier dwellings had a fire in the centre of the main room with the smoke going out through a hole in the roof, so the inside was very smoky, and if the roof leaked, as it often did, drops of sooty water would fall from the ceiling. The smell of burning peat would have served as a universal deodorant, impregnating everybody's clothes. From the end of the 18th century the hearth was usually sited at a gable end. The fire was kept going all the time to keep the place warm and dry, and also because, in the absence of matches, it could be quite difficult to get it started again. The walls were thick, the ceilings low and the roofs well insulated, being covered with turves and thatch, so it must have been quite cosy inside, with plenty of warmth generated by the fire and by the many bodies, animal as well as human. The floor was of bare earth, with mats of grass or rushes laid over it. There wasn't room for much furniture apart from chairs and stools set around the fire, low enough to keep the heads of those sitting on them below the level of the smoke. There were no beds, and people slept on heather piled against a wall and covered by a blanket, or, later, on sacking filled with chaff. Food would be simple, mainly oatmeal, potatoes and turnips, occasionally supplemented by fish and cheese. It would not have been plentiful, and people didn't grow as tall as today. Obesity would not have been a problem at Inninmore. It's surprising the men had the energy for so much hard physical work - tasks such as clearing the meadow of rocks, digging drainage ditches and tilling the soil, all done with simple hand tools, must have been required a great deal of effort and persistence. The women too were expected to join in the manual labour and to carry heavy loads in creels upon their backs. We like to think of the descendants of the folk who lived in such humble dwellings and endured such hardships now prospering and growing taller amid the richer pastures of the New World and the Antipodes.

The present cottage was built in 1862, being one of a series of shepherd's houses of unusually high standard built throughout the estate at the behest of Octavius Smith. Smith had made his money from distilling gin in London, but he was an enlightened man, well ahead of his time in his concern for the welfare of his employees. The employee who lived at Inninmore was called "a watcher" rather than a shepherd, because his principal duty was to keep an eye on that distant part of the estate and to deter poachers, deer-stalking then being of great importance to the proprietor. We know that a succession of watchers lived in the cottage until just before the First World War, when it was vacated. Chubby thinks it then remained unoccupied until Dougie Cameron's parents went to live there in 1931. It was abandoned for a second time a year before the Second World War.

Shipwrecks

Most of the information in this chapter comes from *Argyll Shipwrecks* by Peter Moir and Ian Crawford. It's a fascinating and well-written book, but you shouldn't read it just before you go to sea. There are many wrecks along the Sound of Mull. It's been a marine highway for centuries, and is now well marked with lights, but in bad weather its twisting course and numerous rocky islands and promontories made it hazardous for sailing ships, as it is at any time for a powered vessel with an inattentive helmsman. There's a school for divers in Lochaline, and on most calm days we see small boats anchored near the island and black figures going over the side to look at the wrecks on the seabed nearby.

Two wrecks from the 17th century have been discovered quite close to Inninmore. Both were investigated and written up by Dr Colin Martin, a maritime archaeologist at St Andrews University who has a special interest in the nautical history of Morvern. The earlier of these, though the more recently discovered, in 1991, is the wreck of *HMS Swan*, which foundered off Duart Point in 1653. The *Swan* was a small fast warship built in the reign of Charles 1st and designed to catch pirates in the Irish Sea. The circumstances of her loss are unknown. Many interesting artefacts were recovered from the wreck and are now preserved by the National Museums of Scotland. Before the location of the *Swan* was known we picked up a corroded metal ball about three inches in diameter from among the pebbles on the beach at Craignure. We wonder if it was a cannon ball that over four centuries of tides had worked its way there from Duart.

The second of the historic wrecks is that of *HMS Dartmouth*, a 32-gun frigate 80 foot in length that in the autumn of 1690 was sent, under the command of a Captain Pottinger, to force Maclean of Duart, an ardent Jacobite, to sign articles of allegiance to King William. Legend has it that Maclean, knowing his motley collection of clansmen would be no match for the professional soldiers of the king, summoned the witches of Mull to his aid. The assembled coven conjured up a terrible storm, forcing the *Dartmouth* and her two companion vessels, the *Lark* and the *Fanfan*, to take shelter in Scallastle Bay, which is on the north coast of Mull about four miles west of Duart and almost opposite Inninmore. This bay has always been used as an emergency anchorage, and in bad weather we still see ships of various sizes sheltering there. *Dartmouth* tossed at her anchor for three days waiting for the storm to abate. It would have been too rough to get to and from the shore in a small boat, and the 140 men on board, many of them probably soldiers unaccustomed to the sea, must have had a miserable time, packed together below deck, sea-sick, cold and hungry. On the evening of the third day the anchor cable suddenly parted, and discomfort changed to terror. Even with bare timbers the ship was blown rapidly out of the bay and out into the Sound, where she was exposed to the full strength of the gale. She gyrated as the gusts hit her, and because of her high-sided structure, the standard design for warships of that time, she was pushed over almost to the point of capsize first one way then the other. Assuming she was moving at about five knots, it would have taken her half an hour to be driven the three miles across the Sound. The sailors would have realised they were doomed unless they could quickly gain control, and they must have struggled desperately to put a sea anchor over the stern or perhaps erect a small sail forward. But they were impotent in the violence of the gale. The captain's orders would have been inaudible, and men and gear would have slid on the lurching deck and gone overboard. There was no prospect of help, and all they could see around them would be the white crests of the monstrous waves. Then, amidst the tumult of the wind and water, they would hear a deeper roar, and through the gloom they would be able to make out the foaming of the sea as it crashed onto the land ahead.

The *Dartmouth* was driven inexorably onward until she was thrown against the rocks at the western end of Inninmore Island. Her hull was smashed and she quickly sank. All but a handful of the men on board were drowned. Five survivors somehow managed to make their way to Fort William, the nearest friendly stronghold. Their escape must have been almost as terrifying as the wreck itself. After scrambling onto the rocks, exhausted and helpless, they would have had to evade the wrath of the clansmen living at Inninmore and along their route, who would have known how the *Dartmouth* had been harrying their fellow Highlanders. Perhaps one of them perished at Englishman's Point as he tried to get away. The wreck, which now lies about 20 feet down at low tide, was discovered in 1973. Many of the contents have since been removed for preservation, but enough remains to make for an interesting dive and to merit protected status.

This western end of Inninmore Island faces the prevailing wind and collects all sorts of flotsam, small and large, including at least two other drifting ships. The next ship to go aground there was the small collier *River Tay* in the late 1940s. Few details are available, but it appears that her engine failed as she was going down the Sound and she was blown onto the island. In February 1973 a little steamship called the *Ballista* came to salvage the *River Tay's* cargo of coal, but she too came to grief at the same spot when a gale snapped her moorings. The crew of three scrambled onto the island, where they spent an uncomfortable night until their flares attracted the attention of a passing ferry. For some years the mast and funnel of the *Ballista* remained visible above the water, but now the only readily accessible remnants are the bases of the bunk beds in the cottage (see page 31).

At the other end of Inninmore Island, about a hundred yards out from the Morvern shore, lies the wreck of the iron steamship *Thesis,* length 167 feet, which foundered in October 1889 while carrying a cargo of pig iron from Middlesbrough to Belfast. All the crew escaped. The wreck lies at an angle about 80 feet down, and is a favourite for divers because the hull remains largely intact, there is an abundance of marine life, and there are numerous portholes and other apertures. However the tide runs fast at this point and when flowing strongly can carry an unwary diver away.

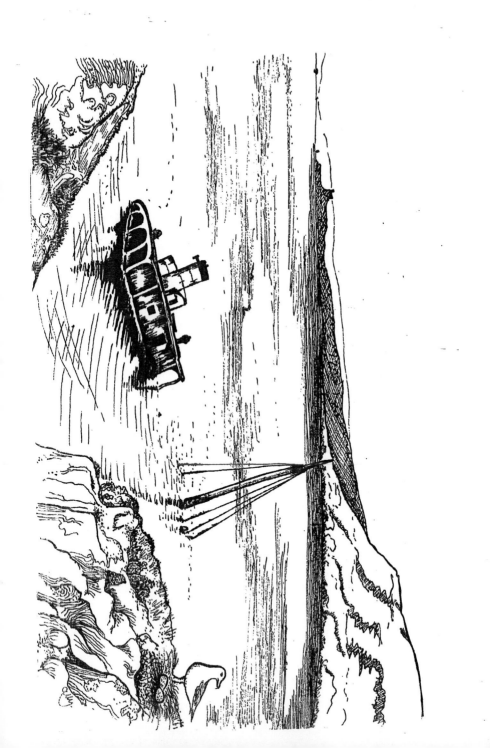

The biggest ship to sink near Inninmore was the Dutch steam cargo vessel *Buitenzorg*, nearly 450 feet in length, which went down in broad daylight in January 1941 (Chubby says it was September) while carrying a mixed cargo from Calcutta. Moir and Crawford suggest she was probably going through the Sound to avoid U-boats when she struck a rock, possibly an outcrop from Inninmore Island, and sank fifteen minutes later a mile to the southeast of Ardtornish Point. All the crew managed to escape. Chubby Ives, then 19 years old, was working with half a dozen companions in the field by Old Ardtornish castle, from which they had a clear view of the whole episode. They came to a very different conclusion about the sinking. Atlantic convoys, bound mainly for Halifax or Murmansk, used to assemble by the island of Lismore up Loch Linnhe, about 30 ships at a time, before being shepherded by destroyers down the Sound of Mull and out through the Minches. U-boats were then taking a horrendous toll, and for merchant seamen the thought of dying in the icy waters of the Atlantic must have been unbearable. A number of merchant ships developed unexplained steering problems and ran aground on Mull before they could get out to sea. The *Buitenzorg* was steaming down the Sound well clear of any rocks when, without explosion or other commotion, she started getting lower in the water and quietly began to sink. The crew launched the lifeboats promptly and all got away before the ship went down. The only possible explanation to those watching from the shore was that she'd been deliberately scuttled, probably by the opening of her seacocks. An incident like this, so demoralising to the war effort, would have been hushed up, and it seems that the truth has never since emerged.

The *Buitenzorg's* cargo included tin, which would be well worth salvaging if the water wasn't so deep. Some of her lighter cargo, latex, floated off and came ashore in our bay. We've found several cubes, about 18 inches square, made up of crinkly layers of crude rubber, yellow-brown in colour. We've tried cutting them up into little pieces as supplementary fuel: the latex burns fiercely but gives off unpleasant black smoke. There are still a few bales half-covered by grass underneath the gorse bushes where they were deposited by high tides and gales, remnants of a trade that was vital during the war but since the advent of synthetic rubber is no longer relevant.

In the deep water just off Ardtornish Point lies the wreck of the Grimsby trawler *Evelyn Rose,* which, just after midnight on 30th December 1954, went hard aground on the rocks just 50 yards from the warning light, even though the weather was calm and clear. She was badly holed and soon slipped down into the depths. It all happened so quickly that only two of the 13 crewmen managed to escape. A scar of red paint from her hull can still be seen on the rocks. The cause of this disaster couldn't be established with certainty, but the trawler had run aground on two previous occasions, and a report of her taking cases of whisky on board at Oban suggests that the helmsman may have been influenced by the imminence of Hogmanay. It was known that, in good weather, after rounding Duart Point skippers of carefree disposition might sometimes set a course down the Sound and go below for a breather.

The richest wreck of all, the Tobermory galleon, hasn't yet been located despite numerous attempts. She was the *Santa Maria de Gracia y San Juan Battista,* a straggler from the Spanish Armada, who was trying to get home round the north coast of Scotland when she put into Mull for repairs. She's said to have sunk in Tobermory Bay following an unexplained explosion. We know, however, that this story was put about to mislead treasure-hunters. What really happened is that, like the *Dartmouth,* she broke from her moorings in a gale, was driven down the Sound and sank near Inninmore. We're sure that one day, when we're out fishing on a calm and sunny afternoon, we'll see the glint of Spanish bullion in the depths.

The last inhabitants

The last people to reside in Inninmore cottage were Dougie and Emma Cameron, who lived there from 1935, when they were married, until 1938, when Dougie was made redundant and they had to move away. This section is taken partly from an interview that Faith Raven recorded with Emma Cameron in 1986 when she was 85 years old, nearly 50 years after she had rowed away from the cottage for the last time, and partly from a long talk I had with Chubby Ives when he too was 85. Memory can play tricks for all of us: our recollections are subtly edited over time to make them more comfortable - or sometimes more colourful - and eventually we come to believe, without any intention to deceive, that the edited version is true. I know that I've been through this process myself, because others have told me that some of my recollections of our early days at Inninmore don't correspond with theirs. However Chubby's memory is renowned for its accuracy and detail, and his family knew the Camerons well. Where the two accounts differ I've put Emma's version in italics.

Emma Joyce grew up in Edinburgh, where her father was a kilt-maker. Dougie spent his boyhood at Drimnin, 15 miles down the coast to the west of Lochaline, where his father was a shepherd. Dougie was a large man, over six foot tall, and he was ten years older than Emma. They met at the house of a mutual friend in Lochaline when Emma, then aged 28, was over from Edinburgh on holiday. She was already engaged to a man from Acharacle, but she fell in love with Dougie, broke off her engagement and within a few months was married to him. *Emma and Dougie met one Saturday evening at a dance in Lochaline, where he had walked from Drimnin. He used to speak Gaelic with his family but conversed in English with his new acquaintance.* Dougie's family were Catholic and Emma converted before their marriage. They married on 25th January 1935 in Oban, where there was a Catholic church. Emma's description of her wedding dress suggests a pleasing blend of femininity and thrift.

Mrs Cameron: I never wanted to be dressed in white. I said I would rather get something that would do me for other dances so I picked a kind of green, very pale green, and a picture hat.

Mrs Raven: You must have looked lovely.

Mrs Cameron: I don't know if I looked lovely but I felt lovely.

Straight after the ceremony they returned to Lochaline on the steamer *Lochinvar* and were driven round to Inninbeg cottage, where they had tea with another (unrelated) family of Camerons. This Mr Cameron preceded Chubby as shepherd, and his daughter Maggie would later become Chubby's wife. At about 7 pm Dougie and Emma walked down to the beach, got into a small boat and set off to row the three miles to Inninmore. The wind was in the north and it was very cold. *Emma hadn't been in a small boat before and she had no idea where they were going.* Dougie's parents and sister had been living in the cottage, having previously moved there from Drimnin, but they vacated it for the newly-weds. It's to be hoped that someone had left some provisions and lit a fire before the bride arrived in the chilly gloom of a winter evening in her pale green dress. Unfortunately Dougie had mislaid the key and he had to break open the door (why on earth had they bothered to lock it?). It was hardly the most blissful prelude to a wedding night.

Emma was ill for a fortnight. Five years after their wedding a man arrived in a boat from the estate bringing their wedding present, a Wedgewood tea service in pink and white. Emma treasured it for the rest of her life.

Dougie now had a job as 'watcher' for the Ardtornish estate, one of his duties being to keep a lookout for poachers. Deer stalking was of great importance at that time, and during the stalking season Dougie would serve as a ghillie, doing various tasks such as disembowelling and transporting the carcases. He sometimes commuted weekly, staying at a bungalow in the estate yard on working days and returning to the cottage at weekends. Emma used to get very lonely and her sister-in-law would go and stay to keep her company.

At the cottage the room to the left was used as a kitchen, as now, but the room on the right was used as a sitting room. The couple slept in the little room at the back, which must have been cramped but very cosy. At bedtime Dougie used to hang his fob watch from a nail in the wall by the bed so that he could tell when it was time to get up. He usually got to the estate by walking along the path to Inninbeg and then going on his motorbike, which he kept there. Legend has it that he used to ride his motorbike along the path to and from the cottage, but Chubby recalls that in fact he rode it there just once, and took so many frights that he brought it back in the boat and never rode it along the path again. The path was in much better condition in those days, with bridges over all the burns. Dougie kept these in good repair, splitting oak trunks to make stout planks. The postman walked down to deliver letters twice a week.

Emma recalled that Dougie had constructed the path himself, and rode down it on his bike most days. He always rode first to Lochaline pier to collect bread and other provisions from the steamer.

They burnt coal rather than wood on the fires. The estate allocated them three tons of coal a year, which was brought round from Lochaline in the grey boat. They didn't have a wireless, and Emma spent the long winter evenings reading novels or knitting. Sometimes she would walk down to Inninbeg to play whist with the other Camerons. It was a long way to walk for a game of cards, but perhaps she used to stay overnight. They kept a cow at Inninmore, which was taken there by boat. Although a city girl Emma learnt how to milk it. This must have been rather a tie, preventing trips away. The cow was fed on hay and turnips and lived in the byre - it was probably the muck of that same cow, well rotted, that I cleared out 50 years later. They also had a pig, whose sty can still be seen behind the cottage, and chickens. In addition Dougie kept two terriers, a cairn and some ferrets to assist in his job of keeping down the foxes. The meadow to the east of the cottage, which they called the croft, was used mainly for hay, but it also had a cultivated patch that grew excellent turnips, potatoes and carrots. Emma recalled helping with the hay-making, which she didn't enjoy – and from my own experience I'd agree that what townees see as a charming country pastime is in reality a strenuous and boring chore. One year a horse was brought along the path to plough the croft. *Dougie used to pull the plough himself, with Emma walking behind to hold it steady.* We came across the plough, rusty and broken, in the bracken behind the cottage. It has two shares of standard size and was clearly intended for a horse. If Dougie indeed pulled it himself he must have been a very strong man.

The burn to the east of the cottage was dammed to make a pool where they could get water and wash clothes. For toileting there was a privy about 30 yards behind the west end of the cottage (not, apparently, the little shed attached to the back of the cottage that we now use for storing wood). A lean-to storage shed abutted the east wall of the byre, and you can still see a line of bitumen where it was joined.

Dougie had a rowing boat, which he winched up on to the pebbles that shelve quite steeply on the eastern half of the bay. The winch, although rusty, was still in working order when we first arrived, but then it disappeared, presumably carried off by a boatman (or two boatmen – it was very heavy) for service elsewhere. Rather surprisingly, although Dougie enjoyed fishing he didn't operate the fish trap. Perhaps in those days no suitable wire netting was available.

Provisions were delivered once a week (*once a month*) by van to Inninbeg. The couple supplemented these with their home-grown vegetables, fish caught in the bay, rabbits taken in snares at Old Ardtornish, where they were plentiful, and scones, which Emma baked on the fire. Outside the front door of the cottage Emma made a small flower garden, fenced off to keep out the deer. Chubby says sheep thieves later used this little enclosure to corral the animals prior to driving them down the beach and loading them onto a boat. The last remnant of Emma's garden, a peony, was still growing in the grass when we came 40 years later, but after a few years it too disappeared, and all that remained was the outline of a cobbled path. The wildlife seems to have been much as it still is today: Emma could recall eagles nesting on the cliffs and seals and otters on the island.

During their time at Inninmore Emma had her first two children, both boys. The maternity arrangements were quite adventurous by Chubby's account and positively horrendous by Emma's, but she seems to have taken it all in her stride. On each occasion, when the baby was due, Dougie rowed her down to Inninbeg, from where she was driven by car to Lochaline to catch the steamer to Oban.

When labour began Emma went by rowing boat all the way to Oban, a distance of at least six miles across water where wind and tide often create tricky currents and choppy waves. Emma insisted on doing her share of the rowing, which was a welcome distraction from the labour pains.

In Oban she stayed with Dougie's family, who'd now moved there, to have the baby. A few days later she came back again, this time on the estate launch. It's perhaps surprising that Emma didn't prefer to stay at the cottage for the births. Unless she had special problems, the risks of home delivery would surely have been less than the risks of giving birth in a small boat on a choppy sea. Perhaps midwifery wasn't one of Dougie's many skills.

Inrinmore
Cottage

Envoi

These episodes and pictures have come flooding into my mind, and all I've had to do is choose the words to set them down. But the unique and numinous spirit of the place can't really be conveyed in words - though perhaps I can give some idea of it by describing what it feels like to be there. After a few days in that clear atmosphere all the petty worries and clutter of modern life melt away, so that the essentials stand out unobscured. Problems you've been worrying over for ages seem to resolve themselves and the ravelled sleeve of care is knitted up. The very process of living becomes reason enough for your existence, and you put your heart into your daily activities instead of regarding them as a chore to be got through before you move on to something more important. You don't regard your stay there as a holiday, or even as an escape or a retreat, but rather as a time when you can live a real life. Although there's no one to admire or criticise your efforts, you do every little task as well as you possibly can, because the place expects it of you. You have to be a jack-of-all-trades, turning your hand to everything. What you don't already know how to do you have to work out from first principles or learn by trial and error. Except when you go on shopping expeditions, which you do as seldom as you can, money languishes in the side pocket of your pack and loses its meaning. If you do have to go to a shop, you feel almost sorry for the mundane life of the other people there. You don't in the least miss the trappings of modern civilisation, and what's going on in the rest of the world no longer seems relevant. There are no electrical gadgets or machines, and the air is free of their noise and smell. There are no screens to watch, and you deal in reality not with images. If you want music you must make it for yourself. You're not at the beck and call of bells, sirens, jingles and bleeps. You luxuriate in simplicity and thrift, gaining satisfaction from doing things in their natural sequence and using as few resources as you can. You look after your tools and other equipment with great care, making them last as long as possible, and when something breaks you don't just throw it away and buy a new one, you set to and mend it, even if it takes all day. You're always aware of the rhythms of the day and of the tides, and you measure out your routines in synchrony with them. You become alert to forthcoming changes in the weather from shifts in the wind and the clouds and from the look of the sky and the sea, and you plan your day accordingly. You don't wear a watch because you do things when you think the time is right, rather than when a dial on your wrist tells you to. Lunchtime isn't one o'clock, it's when you feel like having lunch. You live wholly in the present, without concerns for the past or anxieties for the future. You go to bed early and quickly fall asleep, and your dreams will be unusually vivid.

It's a luxury to be alone at Inninmore. You can do what you please when you please. You can wear what you like. You don't need to shave. You can stand naked in the washtub by the fire without worrying about the neighbours. You can eat with your fingers. You can pee on the lawn in broad daylight, so long as you move around to spread the greening and take care not to hit the little purple beetles that come in July. You can shout obscenities (though you'll seldom feel the need) without upsetting anyone, and you can talk to yourself without fear of being locked up. You can be as tidy or untidy as you like, knowing that you can always lay your hands on things you want because no one will have moved them. Even when you've been on your own for days you don't feel at all lonely. There's no bolt on the door but you've no fear of intruders, and if there are any ghosts you can be sure they'll be benign. When friends appear, once you've come out of your reverie and got over your initial irritation, you feel very warmly towards them and want to give them all your attention. Despite the discomforts and whatever the weather, you feel that this is where you're supposed to be, and that you're a part of nature, not just a user and observer of it. When it's light you can look out and wonder at the beauty of the earth. When it's dark and the skies are clear, you can gaze up at the stars and wonder at the majesty of the universe. Everything you can see gives you faith in everything you can't see. Anxieties and pettiness flee away, and you know you're capable of great things. It's as if here you're transfigured into a being more complete and rounded than your usual self, with body and soul in harmony, just as the place is in harmony with the spirit that pervades it. When the time comes to leave, a pang of sorrow disarms you as you close the front door, and you resolve to come back soon. The aura of the place goes with you as you walk back along the path, and illuminates your being for many days to come.

Extracts from the visitors' book

Here's a specimen of a piece of bark from a carboniferous tree in return for the hospitality. Also a piece of "Inninmorite" – a rock first described from here and named after this place. It forms the rock on the shore.
Martin Warren, 6th July 1973

Called here while canoeing from Taynuilt to Tobermory. Perfect weather. Earlier today we caught and photographed a baby seal and then let it go.
Donald McNaught, 8th July 1975

An afternoon walk down from the castle. Not enough time remains and we're not prepared for staying the night, Goddammit. Bread, cheese and tea, then hot-footin to beat the fading light. Sleeping bags next time. Thanks.
Phil Missellbrock, 28th October 1975

We thought the primroses and violets were almost overdone by Nature's lavish hand. Now in hope of spotting an eagle we stagger upwards
Joanna, 23rd April 1976

Ticks pretty bad, gnats pretty bad, rain pretty bad, otherwise a really superb holiday.
Nicola Robertson, 17th August 1979.

We came, we saw, we fell in love with Inninmore.
Barbara Creighton, 23rd August 1980

Maggie Grizzly Andy Robin & Hercules Big Softy Were Here
2nd July 1981

Time forgotten by time forgetting. Thank you.
P and R, 12th April 1982

Storm force 10 overnight from SSW. Orkney Longliner alright but
Skua sailing dinghy landed up on beach having dragged its mooring
block 60 yards, but fortunately no damage. Mooring block must
weigh 80 lbs +.
Richard Collins, 11th August 1982

Expedition to Oban – Longliner to Craignure and Caledonia to
Oban. Very fine day with good views. Paps of Jura and Colonsay
seen. Opportunity for laundrette and swim. Useful ship's chandlery
– Nancy Black. Mass of fish boxes seen on quay, eternal source of
our furniture
Richard Collins, 13th August 1982

Here, where the basalt meets the granite,
You never thought we'd come; though tempted
By winter fireside descriptions
Of your other Eden, demi-
Paradise, we never made it quite.

Then, rainy Bank Holiday, August eighty-two
Sickness kept us from two rendez-vous
By Ardtornish Point; but two days late
From Yorkshire we shoved our way via Lomond,
Tossed over Onich, guided by Claggan,
Heartened the long lane in evening sun
Till squelched to a stop at the steadings
For an overnight "rest" in the car.

Downcast by rain, wind and weighty pack,
We found the track by wife's Man-Friday eyes;
Slithered, climbed, ducked and fell, swore and stopped,
And wondered why in middle age the spirit
Could no longer force the failing flesh.

But, Browning (and Bacons) the best was
Still to come. Though wearied, wet and weak
The 'eadmaster's face at last appeared
To astound Celly's eyes idly peering,
Unbelieving, through the window. No!

Yes!! 'Twas indeed the Duttons sang:
"We made it
Through the rain, and stayed two days,
To find your other Eden all you'd said
To be: a charged existence: restoring solitude.
Derek Dutton, 1st September 1982

....celebrated Christmas together. Warm, wet, full-moon nights, pork
and Christmas cake, and not at all the Spartan Christmas that we'd
boasted to our friends about. No visitors, apart from the regulars
(deer, seals, eagles), but a very good way of focusing on (as well as
escaping from) Christmas. The wood shed is stocked with very wet
wood. We are just getting into the groove, and the five days have
gone. Esther (2) thinks it's all magic, and so do we.
Mike Downham, 29th December 1982

Back-packed from Craignure, footsore and weary, and about 30
secs of daylight left. Decided to stay.
Bryan Eadie, 5th April 1983

....what I loved most about this place was the complete (or almost
complete) isolation. The expression "getting away from it all" was
created for this place. We had two groups of visitors at the weekend,
though. The second shared their squat lobster, velvet crab and
dogfish with us: all were delicious, especially the dogfish. .... I'm
looking out across the bay once more in the early morning light –
it's so beautiful, shrouded in mist. Time to brag: I was the only one
who spotted the eagle, and who swam in the sea. Boy, was it cold?
Yes, it was cold, very. Freeze the gorbals off ye. Nasty.
Mark Payne, 11th July 1983

Sunday morning,.. and time to go. It will be very difficult to revert
to reality. Sitting at the table, looking across the slow-moving misty
Sound of Mull, it seems as this is the only place left in the world,
and we the only living things. Those silent sailing ships and distant
lights are mere apparitions. Thank you for a few long moments of
tranquillity.
Richard Westlake, 1st October 1983

Dear Mouse,

Why, when there's so much other good food around, do you have to chew pieces out of the apples I've carried on my back along the path? And why do you especially like to leave your mark in the porridge bowls, so that I have to get cold washing them before breakfast? And why do you wake me at 4 a.m. by scampering over my pillow, and when I light a candle to scare you away, why do you come and peep at it so boldly?

Yours sincerely,
Chris

DEAR CHRIS,

THIS IS MY HOUSE, AND I'LL DO AS I PLEASE. YOU'RE JUST AN INTERLOPER.

YOURS SINCERELY,
MOUSE.
23rd April 1984

Certainly the journey through the wood along the path, across drying waterfalls with boulders deposited in full flow, so to speak, would not be one to bring one's ageing maiden aunt along for a Sunday school stroll but to hobbits this did not prove so problematic, though it was a wearisome and sometimes perilous adventure. John had to negotiate slipping rocks, sloping straight down to the sea in order to retrieve his sleeping bag which had bounced softly down into the slow stream. The spiders and midgets which descended on us as we battled our way through the luscious undergrowth, had by the time we reached Inninmore sunk their mandibles into our flesh and decided to be ticks instead. Memories of "The African Queen" (though leeches were the horrors there) and John Donne's "The Flea" seemed to be appropriate imagery on which to contemplate, particularly as our nightly ritual of bodily investigation took on a highly important significance.
Then there has been Bunny, who has accompanied us on our excursions into the hills to find the loch at the top. He became very

*excited when we came close to three red deer and when John
responded by raising the antler he had found to his brow. He saw
lizards too and a small frog and absorbed the colours and smells of
all the flowers which festooned the countryside. One night he
escaped from my pocket (so great was his excitement) but John
discovered him on the beach lying near a pile of driftwood, gazing
up at the pink night sky. We scooped him up and took him back to
the cottage lying softly on the bay with the candlelight licking soft
shadows on the walls and the wonderful furniture. The fire burning
with intense heat gave us all much pleasure and the kettle too,
though blackened with smoke, it sang and burbled happily on its
hook. Bunny was tired by now so John put him to bed, a matchbox
for his pillow and a piece of toilet paper for a sheet. We too
crawled off wearily to sleep, the lights of the odd boat and of
Craignure and the lighthouse flickering gently beneath the night
stars. No one called to visit us for tea or a glass of wine, only the
seals raised their heads above the water to check us out. And now
today, we must leave all this, the view from the front door step must
be savoured for the last time ....well perhaps not quite the last time*
Winky Medley, 21st May 1984

*Made it with bike – one heck of a carry, along coast route with
rocks – by 8.20 p.m. Venison steak (from beast killed by car) plus
onions, rolls, cocoa and whisky, with rice pud and blackberry jam.
In this way I celebrate my 56th birthday.*
Bernard Heath, 29th September 1984

*In the bay is a solitary curlew, tired of emotional entanglements,
complaining mournfully at intrusions. By night the moon fixes the
earth with a frost that the day's wan sun cannot loose.*
Chris Bacon, 1st January 1985

*It was fun taking it in turns to make the porrige. When the girls
made it it was all hard and lumpy and when the boys made it it was
runny and watery.*
Laura Bacon, 29th May 1985

*It was very good fun when we came to Inninmore. I liked it when we
went to the Table of Lorne. It was pouring with hail stones but on*

the way back it was boiling hot and my foot fell into a deep mud.
Good bye.
Alex Bacon, 29th May 1985

Motored from Lochaline, caught mackerel and cuddies. Ate the
mackerel and gave the cuddies to the gulls. Had a lovely day. But
where is the toilet?
The Livingstones, 30th July 1985

Slow the time and slow the tide,
Slow the cloud caps drift and bide,
Slow the stream and slow the dream,
At Innnmore my heart has been.

Strong the cliffs stand sentinel,
Rampart wide the crumbling fell.
Sea rocks greet the gentling sea
Holding fast the heart of me.

Silent the seal and silent the deer
Silent the eagle's drift and steer,
Silent too the call of the Sound,
Still the heart this place has found.
Graham Hellier, 30th October 1985

We came and first footed you – but you were out! Happy New Year!
Quin and Dave, 1st January 1986

We walked in by the middle path. The moon, affronted by last
night's eclipse, lashed the earth with hail and capped the Mull hills
with the first snow of winter. We pick blackberries with numb
fingers, and hear a stag roaring on the tops. The rowans at
Achranich are already chattering with redwings.
Chris Bacon, 18th October 1986

Snow on the Mull hills, but a ringed plover already sitting on four
eggs on the shingle beyond the gorse bushes. In the bay, a solitary
great northern diver, and a gaggle of 50 shags, circling and
displaying in the choice of a mate, like at a disco. We painted the

outside of the window, and made a new stone seat, where a slow worm promptly took up residence.
Chris Bacon, 18th April 1987

I walked two thirds of the path. It was slow work stopping to sweep the leaves. I moved lots of stones. I helped cut poles for the fish trap. I saw the clarabels running on the beach and planted potatoes in the garden. I thought I'd better watch out in case Goldilocks came to the cottage, so I ate all my porridge up quick.
John Bacon, 19th April, 1987

Inninmore, Inninmore,
Home of men and mice.
Inninmore, Inninmore,
You are awfully nice.
Eagles in the cliffs,
Otters on the shore,
Inninmore, Inninmore Inninmore.

Inninmore, Inninmore,
Tranquil by the sea.
Inninmore, Inninore,
You're the place for me,
Climbing in the hills,
Walking on the moors,
Inninmore, Inninmore, Inninmore.

Inninmore, Inninmore,
Heron, deer and seals.
Inninmore, Inninmore,
Cockles for your meals.
The food is always rich
Even if you're poor,
Inninmore, Inninmore, Inninmore.

Inninmore, Inninmore,
Now we have to go.
Inninmore, Inninmore,
Here's a cheerio.

Now our song is done
We'd like to sing some more,
Inninmore, Inninmore, Inninmore.

(to be sung by massed choirs to tune of "Robin Hood")
Lucy Robertson, 19th July 1987

One night the others went out fishing. They said they would only be
out for an hour but they were two hours 40 minutes. Here is a list of
what we felt: tilly-conked, grumpy, annoyed, boared, dark, cold,
frustrated, hungrey, thirsty, no cumpainy, gone out, left, lonely,
cross, ansus, etc. I wont go anymore but when they came back they
had caught 11 fish so we did feel slightly happy.
Becky Rayner, 4th August 1987

We came over in a boat for a picnic tea and found this delightful
cottage and being an inquisitive bunch we tried the door and it
wasn't locked. We went in and found everything one could wish for
if shipwrecked on a desert island. Can we come back soon please?
Emma Chegre, 11th October 1987

I capsized the canoe, the water was lovely and warm and tasted of
beer, and there were 123 naked dancing ladies on the beach.
Paul Spencer, 28th October 1987

My idea of a heaven is no keys, no money and lots of primroses –
this is the nearest I'll probably get! Thank you.
Sylvia Kerr, 2nd May 1988

Went up to waterfall, lost Edward, found a vole and a frog, then,
unfortunately, found Edward.
A friend, 31st May 1988

I made a dinosaur and Frances bashed it down. I fell in the burn
and wetted all my clothes. Had my first go in the canoe. Ate lots of
food. Laura read to me – my best books are Mr Magnolia, Tiny Tim
and Burglar Bill.
John Bacon, 11th June 1988

For the first time ever sunburn beat midges as a source of
complaint. Glad to see the front lawn well mown and fertilised by
Anton's sheep, and to see ringed plovers and sandpipers back in
larger numbers.
Chris Bacon, 11th June 1988

Sat musing on Yeats' poem Innisfree "..for I shall have some peace
there, for peace comes dropping slow…" just as it does here at
Inninmore. Collected firewood and B baked bread and flapjacks.
Walked along the beach and marvelled at rock pools – anemones
and seaweeds – pondered on the rocks – pinks, greys, the lichens
and the gentle lap of the sea. Found yellow wort. Stag silhouette on
crags 9.30 p.m. Warm all-over wash in the bath. Teachers laced
with finest burn water. As usual nothing on TV. Bed.
Michael, 15th June 1988

It's not often that man's coming adds to the beauty and tranquillity
of the natural surroundings. This cottage is one of those rare
examples. Thank you.
Chris Thompson, 25th May 1989

We came but have to go now. Moan moan.
Phil and Caroline, 10th June 1989

Amazingly peaceful. Just us and 200,000,000 midges. Panned for
gold but didn't find any. Hope to be back.
Bill Sibard, 18th June 1989

A U.F.O. and one small mouse
Do hang about this little house.
We saw them both quite late at night,
It almost gave us quite a fright.

The sceptics put it down to gin,
Or M.O.D. or some known thing.
But we know what we saw alright
And we will check it out tonight.

So if this entry is the last

That you see in this scrawl
You'll know that we have been beamed up
And we'll be watching you all.
Jackie, 4th July 1989

It is the evening of the day
I sit and watch the midges play.
Flying insects I can see
All after me.
I sit and watch as midges fly-y-y-y-y.

I've tried Autan and Jungle Juice
And they are just no xxxxing use.
On my body, in my hair,
They make me swear.
I sit and watch as midges bite.

And then the clegs come out as well.
They are attracted by my smell.
They bite me everywhere,
They just don't care.
I sit and watch as midges fly-y-y-y-y.

(to the tune of "As tears go by" by the Rolling Stones)
Dave, 7th July 1989

We sheltered in the cottage, collected stones and waited for the
waves to die down.
Joseph Gaskell, 22nd August 1989

Over looking for a boat that blew away from our fish farm on Mull.
H.Edwards, 21st October 1989

We managed the walk-in in almost record time – little over four
hours!! But despite being cold and wet, with nine of us in here we
soon warmed up – kneeling! After that we had excellent weather –
snow on Mull, and one heavy frost here (the top of Loch Aline
frozen) but blue skies and beautiful sunsets. Lots of skinny-dipping
in sub-zero temperatures, lashings of porridge for breakfast and

*loads of beany hash for supper. Long evenings were spent plaiting
hippie dreads to annoy Granny over Christmas. Clodagh managed
to acquire ticks even in mid-winter – because she's lovely! We're
off today, back to the real world, a broken oil sump and Christmas.*
Rebecca McCowen, 22nd December 1989

*If ever you fancy a weekend away from it all come and stay in
Toxteth. Thanks for the use of the house.*
Glynn, January 1990

*The prospect of a week of Paul's cooking and Owen's imaginative
use of language and Nick's bottom and James' prowess in bed
managed to persuade me to avoid certain death by stupidity/bad
luck/big waves.*
George Bacon, 8th April 1990

*I've just nicked all the valuables in this house so there! I bet you're
wondering where I come from. Well, I come from Leeds and if you
are handsome, charming, lot of money, my phone no is (psss) tell
you later!*
Nicola Ferrie, 16th April 1990

*I pay poll tax of £460 a year for this cottage. Lord Home, who
enjoys all the services all the year round, pays £220 for his mansion
and estate. But maybe he can't stand in his front door in his pyjamas
and watch the otters playing on the rocks.*
Chris Bacon, Easter 1990

*Engine broken so put in to repair. Delightful establishment. The sun
setting, the long shadows defining the contours of Mull, peace and
tranquillity. How clever you are to find a part of heaven so close to
home.*
Jonathan Miles, 28th June 1990

*Walked in from Ardtornish. Great difficulty in finding path at
Inninbeg, man-eating bracken, but once on it no problem. It would
have been beautiful but for the continuous rain. Many times the
family would have turned back, crossed many burns in spate, but we
were glad we reached Inninmore. We were not sure if it was a*

*ruined cottage or whether we would be able to get in or not. Were
we glad when we found not only that we could get in, we felt
welcome, and were able to get a fire going to dry out – what luxury.
... Before I leave let me share a wee poem with you*

*Some folk like to sit on ithers
Because they're kin' a wee.
But I'm a wee Scots jaggy thistle
And naebody sits on me.*
Bob, 7th July 1990

*So hot yesterday that we couldn't bear to go outside so we went
fishing from the kayaks. No mackerel down here yet seemingly, but
we had previously caught quite a few off Canna and Muck. I had a
very alarming and upsetting experience while fishing off the point.
The hand line went tight suddenly and I thought it had snagged
bottom. I paddled in the opposite direction to try and free it when a
small seal surfaced downwind with what looked like a red
moustache. I quickly realised that it had taken a mackerel feather
and was well and truly hooked. What to do? I decided the only
option to limit further risk to the seal was to somehow get it to the
side of the kayak and cut off the hook just above the eye. It was
heart-rending to have to play the seal like a huge fish with it
sporadically surfacing and staring with wild eyes before panicked
thrashing and diving. Its mother looked on from about 20 yards.
Eventually I managed to pull the pup up as gently as possible and
cut off the line. The seal took off with its moustache flapping. If I
hadn't done this the remaining hooks and weight on the trace would
have inevitably snagged or been swallowed, probably killing the pup
. I never thought a seal would take a fishing lure but obviously
common seal pups' curiosity sometimes gets the better of them. I
had not seen the mother and pup approach or I would have been
more wary. I write this to alert people to this danger when fishing
from a canoe or rowing boat, which seem to fascinate seals by their
silent motion.*
Dan Trotter, July 1990

*We have had three full and happy days at Inninmore. This really is a
magical place – it even has ferries at the bottom of the garden!*

Julia Bishop, 7th October 1990

It's been a week of thrushes. Gangs of blackbirds, peppered with song thrushes, squeaking round the blackberries. A pair of mistle thrushes guarding the berry-laden hawthorn. Drifts of fieldfares and redwings passing eastwards beneath the cliffs. And higher up the burn a lingering pair of ring ouzels.
Chris Bacon, 25th October 1990

I should like to suggest, from observations made at Inninmore, why the cuckoo has such a distinctive call and appearance. You might have expected that a bird that depends for procreation on laying its eggs unobserved in the nests of others would be unobtrusive in every way. Yet the cuckoo is exactly the opposite. I suggest that its loud and ludicrous call and its hawk-like appearance actually help it to find the nests of its victims and to lay in them without their noticing. As the cuckoo flies about calling it will inevitably attract the attention of any small birds such as pipits who are nesting nearby; they will fly out to mob it because of its hawk-like appearance, thereby betraying the approximate locality of their nests. Subsequent careful observation will pinpoint the nest precisely. Then, in the second phase of the plan, the male cuckoo will fly past once more, calling loudly, so that both parent pipits will pursue him, leaving their nest unguarded long enough for the female to slip in and lay her egg. Without a manoeuvre such as this it is hard to imagine how the cuckoo could infiltrate a nest replete with eggs that is likely to be watched closely by the parents.
Chris Bacon, 30th May 1991

Walked over from Lochaline. A day of strong winds yet beautiful skies in between showers added to a most enjoyable walk through. A lot is on my mind at the moment and the chance to be alone with my thoughts has helped. I need to go away now and put my period of thinking to good and proper use. Yes, I guess one day I will marry her! Watch this space in the future! Many thanks for a nice stop off and really terrific place.
Peter Braidwood, 9th July 1991

Two black-throated divers and I fished for trout in Mam a'
Chullaich as the sun went down. They caught plenty, with grace and
ease. I got two, without either.
Chris Bacon, 1st August 1991

I've been writing in the visitor's book for years, seven times in fact,
and I've always racked my brains for something witty to say. So, just
to break with tradition, I shall write a short and uninteresting
playlet.
The scene: a storm rages outside, a body lies in the middle of the
floor, Holmes and Watson are deep in debate.
Holmes: We must deduce as much information as possible from the
facts available. Can you tell me how long the victim has been dead?
Watson: Er, well, it's awfully difficult without knowing the cause of
death. However ....
Holmes: If I could tell you rigor mortis has set in would that help?
Watson: Er, yes, it would mean the corpse is about 30 minutes old.
But how can you tell?
Holmes: I can't, it was just a lucky guess.
George Bacon, 21st September 1991

We visited this tranquil spot once again. However, we had to leave
fairly quickly owing to Frankie and his ominous line "Get off the
spaceship."
Owen, 10th April 1992

Note for horticulturalists: boiling water is not good for lawns.
Anon, Easter 1992

Weather forecast very poor. Gale warnings Malin and Hebrides.
The Sound looks like a washing machine. Have decided to make the
most of the tranquillity and stay one more day. Last night stags were
rutting in the field across the burn – lots of noise and this morning
plenty of tracks and torn grass.
C.Griffin, 14th October 1992

Lucy and Andy's Hogmanay dinner

Starter

*Thai hot and sour chicken soup simmered with lemon grass, coconut
and galangal, and liberally sprinkled with chopped fresh coriander.*

Intermission
A small dram

Main course
*Piquant lamb chops with mushroom fried rice (chops marinaded for
24 hours in garlic, rosemary and olive oil).*

Dessert
A selection of fresh fruit
Swiss chocolate
Stilton (if required).

Ample hot toddies until bedtime.
Lucy Robertson, 31st December 1992

*I enjoyed it here playing with my dog and my frisby. Me and my Dad
cept beating my Mum and sister at playing Scrabble. I couldn't get
to sleep some times because my sister was snoring.*
John Bacon, 10th April 1993

LOST: INNINMORE TED
*A reward will be given to eny person who finds him. Last seen on
shelf. Description: light brown, one ear missing, quite small,
probably lonely. Please return to Inninmore if found.*
(picture)
*You are stupid if you've burnt him or take him home because he
belongs here.*
Frances Rayner, 10th April 1993

*Having canoed from Oban we felt in need of a short break on the
shores of this tranquil bay. Sadly we seem to have arrived during a
power-cut and water shortage. The facilities for the disabled are far
from adequate. The Sound of Mull and its adjacent lakes are devoid
of fish and some bizarre virus is killing the deer population. To top
it all our moules were populated by a multitude of pearls. Unable to*

enjoy our usual standard of London cuisine we had to make do with
the following (as an example):

Starter
Pate de foie gras
Salmon mousse
Dressed crab
Moules marinieres

Intermission
A small dump

Main course
Smoked venison in rich red wine and wild mushroom sauce
Clubbed seal a la king with poached golden eagle eggs
An otter surprise (with lemon in its mouth)

Dessert
Jellied seal/fox pups (subject to seasonal variation)
Crispy aromatic swan and custard

Ample hot partner swapping 'til morn
Aidan Bolger, 15th April 1993

Should have a four star classification rather than the AA Guide
suggested five. Room service and restaurant damned good despite
the en suite bathrooms being a little elusive. Found transportation
to this exotic spot a trifle damp and the boat wallah speaking a
strange tongue, although local game shooting jolly good sport.
Found the rush hour crowds somewhat uncomfortable.
Exceptionally fine mineral water when strained carefully through
one's teeth to remove excess debris. Dribble, blurb, snort.
Anon, 31st April 1993

We climbed up through the bracken
And slid back down the hill,
But when the bites and bruises fade,
The memory never will.
Tony, 28th August 1993

Had a great time, so wrote you a poem about an eagle:

He clasps the crag with crooked hands;
Close to the sun in lonely lands,
Ring'd with the azure world, he stands.

The wrinkled sea beneath him crawls;
He watches from his mountain walls,
And like a thunderbolt he falls.
Alfred (Lord) Tennyson, 1st April 1994

We had a lovely picnic chez vous. I am afraid the Auld Alliance
cracked and we had a fearsome Fairy Liquid fight. I hope that we
have left enough for les vaisailles.
Ronald Maclean, 10th July 1994

Passing through on a run, Ardtornish – Inninmore – Loch Tearnait
– Ardtornish. I'm glad I brought my compass. The bracken is 6'
high (I'm 5').
Roger Boswell, 15th July 1994

"We have to walk from the car," she said, "it's a lovely walk."
Well, I'm 51, fat and extremely unfit. 8 waterfalls later, several
large foot blisters, a severely bruised sternum (impaled on a rock in
a raging waterfall), an almost cracked pelvic girdle, soaking feet
and lower body, several pulled shoulder muscles from a too heavy
rucksack, we arrived. I now know in a most profound sense what the
two most irritating words in the English language are: in response
to the question "How far?" the reply "Not far." Anyway we have
arrived. My resolve never to speak again dissolved as soon as I
looked around and saw the quite extraordinary beauty of the place.
Particularly after drying out by a proper fire and the consumption
of ½ bottle of whisky. This is a place one could happily die in and be
re-absorbed into the natural world. It makes me realise the
quintessential silliness of the urban, consumptive and trivial life we
normally lead.
Charles, 31st August 1994

Two great nights spent here. Went for a run along the cliff top and found an injured hill runner lying on his back in a burn. It was me. I had to pick myself up and carry on limping. OK now though.
Roger Boswell, 24th November 1994

For all you medics reading this I offer the following extract from an obscure Scottish medical textbook I picked up recently:

"A wonderful thing is the human kidney.
Most people have two,
But Sidney did nae."

Whilst out wooding in the rain today the muse struck and produced the following

I will arise and go now
And go to Inninmore.
There's a small cabin built there
Of stone and driftwood made.
Nine been tins will I have
And a hole for a lavatree,
And I will live alone there
In the sea-loud glade.
Wynn Bishop, 13th February 1995

... On the last part of the path I surprised several deer, which on seeing me took off up the hill. When I got to the place they'd been standing one deer still remained. She was lying on her back and even when she saw me she seemed unable to get up. The strange thing is, I'd only been thinking a little earlier how nice it would be if I were to stumble across an injured deer, then I wouldn't have to eat that tin of goulash. Anyway I approached the animal very slowly so as not to alarm her, talking to her all the time (Dr Doolittle style). I stroked her for a while to calm her down and then tried to find out what was wrong. One leg seemed to be stuck under her body. I decided to try and move the leg, which she allowed me to do, and thinking it must be broken I went off to find a stick to splint it with, then intending to tether the animal and go and fetch someone to help me get her to a vet. I was about 20 feet away when she got up on all

fours and trotted off down the hill. I must admit I sat for a while shaking my head, wondering whether I'd been dreaming.
Paul Machell, 1st April 1995

What can I say at finding such a spirit-raising bothy not only open but in a superb way? After the rat and rubbish infested dens of the Cairngorm and Glencoe areas, it's an amazing surprise in this day and age. I hope that the tenants' decision to open up their home like this isn't going to prove misplaced faith in their fellow creatures. This is the best open bothy I have seen this side of the North Sea ... I hope it will be here for generations to come.
Ian Barker, 8th May 1995

Called in on our round Mull trip in the Wayfarer. Spent a very comfortable night and saw three otters feeding at the rock. Midge count was fairly low. 31 today – happy birthday to me! Thank you.
Mike Redmond, 8th July 1995

Please try and get some new furniture and give this place a bloody clean. And get a TV, washing machine and telephone. I mean, show some consideration, you slovenly bunch of tykes.
Wee Dougie, 3rd September 1995

Hello there, visitor's book, Georgie here. Now, I've probably been here more than any of you – apart from my parents, and that's only because by chance they were born before me – so I have also read more visitor's book entries than any of you. And after twenty five years it seems to me that they are becoming a little repetitive. Let's face it, we all know Inninmore is a crackin' place. I can see it's magical, wonderful, beautiful, perfect, Scottish, etc, etc. And so can the other people reading this book. So there's not a lot of point telling us that, 'cos we know. So how about a bit of originality with the entries? Take it as read that if you are writing in this book that you think this place is magical, etc, etc. How about something new, or personal to yourself? What are your hopes, fears and dreams? What ridiculous thoughts did you muse upon as you looked at the sea? How often did you go to the field? Were you idiotic enough to dig a sod out of the front lawn? (who was that, for Haggis' sake – own up you prat).

George Bacon, 20th September 1995

Last night and the night before, in the small hours, I saw a comet. It was close to the pole star and appeared to be heading northwest. Its aura surrounded it, ahead and to the sides as well as behind, so that it made a blunt-headed trail in the sky, about half the moon's diameter in width and five moon's diameters in length. Today week is Good Friday.
Chris Bacon, 28th March 1996

Briefly in view at the same time, our smallest and largest birds. In the gorse bushes, a pair of goldcrests. Above the cliff, an eagle swooping in display.
Today I saw a sea eagle for the first time, flying above the wood towards Englishman's Point, then across the Sound to Mull.
Chris Bacon, 31st March 1996

At around noon on Good Friday I set the hill on fire........ (for the rest of this entry see chapter entitled "Fire")
Chris Bacon, 8th April 1996

This place is going to profoundly affect the rest of our lives.
Iggy and Penny, 19th May 1996

Hello to whoever comes here after me. I've walked from the ruined castle along the path, cutting down onto the rocks, and finally arrived here with my two German shepherd dogs, Sasha and Jazz. What a beautiful place. So peaceful and quiet, save for the panting of the dogs. I'll stay an hour or two and then sadly return to the castle. Maybe one day I'll return.
Sue, Sasha and Jazz, 10th September 1996

A wild cat kitten, about half-grown, has kept me company at a safe distance, drinking milk from a saucer and eating scraps outside the window. Three eagles on the cliff, a dipper by the burn and a loon in the bay.
Chris Bacon, 22nd October 1997

I brought Anne here to propose to her, hoping that the magic of the place would act in my favour. Well, no sooner than we were installed, a storm descended, blowing water down the chimney onto our precious store of dry wood and big bits of soot down into the food I'd cooked, dripping on the bed at night, cutting off all views out and flooding the streams so that getting out was an impossibility. They say if the carrot doesn't work, the stick might, but this wasn't what I had hoped for. Climbing a mountain was out, a pilgrimage to the little waterfall at the end of the beach too (Nile delta in between) and soon the cottage was almost moated. Things were going to have to come to a head. I took my heart in my (sodden) boots and asked the question as we shared a bowl of powdered milk. She said "Yes."
Angus Forbes, 3rd April 1997

You may not think it much, but the sheep and I are rather fond of the lawn. Originally it was all bumps and tussocks, but over the years we have steadily chewed away at the tussocks and removed the rocks, we have cropped the grass short with our molars and with our bill-hook, we have nurtured it with solid and liquid fertiliser, until finally we produced the magnificent greensward you see today. So it offends our horticultural sensitivities to find it defaced with large black and brown patches. Lawns don't like having bonfires lit on them, or even having boiling water poured on them. So please try and keep it green. Anyone for croquet?
Chris Bacon, April 1997

Everyone knows that the seals are in league with the sheep that roam the hillside. Shortly after spotting a young seal, the sheep, two in number, strolled up to the front of the cottage. The young seal had informed the sheep that the show might be late that evening as "there are people in the cottage." You see as soon as the lights go out in the cottage the seals haul their equipment (hoops, plinths, platforms, and old-style squeezy car horns) up to the beach. Having set up their equipment on the beach and set fire to some of their stunt hoops, the show begins. The younger seals show off their acrobatic skills while the older ones will balance a ball on their noses or play "The saints come marching in" with seven pals on

synchronised car horns. The sheep watching all the time from their
ringside beach seats. ...
Sam Hawkes, 21ˢᵗ July 1997

The tweetie-birds are so cute. I love them.
Sharon, 4ᵗʰ September 1997

Yacht Tramontane. Have sailed past many times and promised
myself that one day I would stop and visit. Today is that day! Very
nice peaceful place. Will return some day by kayak.
Ian Matheson, 3ʳᵈ June 1998

Peter and Chris came to play Scrabble. Peter won. At teatime a cock
pheasant walked along the beach.
Chris Bacon, 23ʳᵈ June 1998

And lo! There came from beyond the bracken six figures of great
mystery and strange trousers ... They were Captain Pierre Jacques
Pantalon of the Most Ridiculous Trousers, Danny Wrongwellies of
the Most Terrorised Sheep (who was the ship's cook), Duncan
McBiskitts of the Most Brave Sort who never once complained about
his ingrowing toenail, Mary McHairybumpkin of the Fiddler's
Elbow and the Shot Putt Thrower's Arm, Fanny McAdams of the
Abnormal Intelligence (Oh, sweet Fanny McAdams) and Shorty
McNolegs of the Diminutive Persuasion. And it was good. And they
played crazy boules with much gentlemanly etiquette and many
sporting and formal gestures. And it was good. And they played
wonderful music, including Groovy Kind of Love and Kumbaya. And
it was good.
Anon, 19ᵗʰ July 1998

<u>*Lines written on discovery of the loss of his Wellington boots:*</u>

The reason I'm shivering in soaking wet socks
When I've walked in the rain on the fell is
That someone broke into my old clothing box
And then buggered off in my wellies.

If he'd taken my trousers I wouldn't have cared.

My old pair of sandals as well is
Superfluous footwear I'd gladly have spared.
The one thing I need is my wellies.

One day he will drown while traversing the mire,
And wherever the worst part of hell is,
His legs will be roasted in brimstone and fire,
Those legs that walked off in my wellies.

(OK, I know it's crummy, but you try finding rhymes for "wellies")
Chris Bacon, 12th August 1998

A rainy two weeks which concentrated our energies on rebuilding
the bedroom fireplace. In between we watched an otter crunching
crabs on the beach, the gannets catching fish in the bay and the
terns carrying fry. The first time we've visited without any children.
Heather Bacon, 20th August 1998

The midges and rock formations remind me of happy family
camping weekends in the Magaliesberg mountains in South Africa.
Maybe the sense of security and comfort comes from a memory
trace of the best place for our Stone Age ancestors to be.
Tessa McArdle, 30th August 1998

The lament of your wellies in such crummy rhyme
Reminds me perhaps that they could have been mine.
I bought them in Oban in '79,
More like 11 than tiny size 9.
However I join you in damning the crime
Of buggering off in our wellies.
Richard Collins, 17th October 1998

The Morvern postie walked from Ardtornish. Nice day. Heard a lot
about this spot. Think it's beautiful, but glad I haven't to deliver
letters every day.
Catherine Cameron, 20th December 1998

Absolutely brilliant, as ever. Managed to spot some seals and a
naked man in the sea. Somewhat strange.

Jam, 2nd January 1998

*James MacNeil and Kevin Lindsey walked from Lochaline and
stayed the night. James drives a Chieftain tank, but didn't bring it
this time.*
Chris Bacon, 4th April 1999

*Had a great time. It was a bit cold though. We made a snowman as
tall as me (about 4-5 feet).*
Lotti Hughes, 16th April 1999

*Finally managed to fight our way through the jungle to get here. I
had forgotten how bad the bracken gets on the path during summer.
It feels a bit surreal enjoying Inninmore without the aid of alcohol.
It makes chopping wood a little less hazardous but the midges a
little more annoying. I'm sure to be back again on foot (not like
those cheats who use boats) but I'll napalm the path first.*
Alex Bacon, 22nd August 1999

*An osprey hovered briefly over the fish trap before departing for
Africa.*
Chris Bacon, 15th October 1999

*I wish to register a complaint. The fire and griddle were
insufficiently large to cook my three companions side by side. Was
forced to dismember them with my Swiss army knife first, a tedious
process. Do come and have lunch with me some time.*
H.Lecter MD, 20th October 1999

*I came along a fabled path
Above a fabled shore,
To reach, through fabled wood, at last
The fabled Inninmore.*

*Now fables often tell the truth
Then add a little more.
But truth beats fable every time
At fabled Inninmore.*
Jim McKenna, 31st January 2000

135 yards of path cleared. By God we sweated and blistered
porridge, whisky and tears for that.
George Bacon, 28th March 2000

The deep peace of the rhythmic tide to you,
The deep peace of the running stream to you,
The deep peace of the earth and sky to you,
The deep peace of the creating God to you.
Liz Styan, 9th June 2000

Sailed here today. Lovely to be here, where our great great uncle
Alan and his wife Ann McMaster reared their nine children, in the
mid to late 19th century. His name was Alan Morrison.
Margaret McAllister, 2nd July 2000

I'm passing through on a charity walk for Macmillan Nurses Cancer
Relief from Sheffield to Taransay ....Total distance is about 500
miles, and I've diverted here from Fort William for a few days, and
will then continue to Mallaig, cross to Skye, walk to Uig, and then
take a ferry to Tarbert on Harris ....
Howard Parry, 12th July 2000

First time on my friend's yacht, decided to investigate paradise –
and it is! Lottery win buys this place, have already converted it into
retreat for retired donkeys. You'll all still be welcome. Bring hay!
Andrew, 20th July 2000

Waking up in my attic room, shared with the friendly bat, sluicing
down every morning in an icy burn and soothing midge bites,
blasted showers in waterfalls and mussels for starters, two weeks of
log-chopping, fire-starting, rip-cording, whisky-drinking fun just
isn't long enough.
Eric Langley, 10th August 2000

Well, looking out over the Sound to the mysterious Mull (completely
covered in a sheet of cloud – what's over there? I've never found
out despite it being August), and listening to the bleating of the
sheep out on the lawn (always came back, despite being chased over

the burn), it's hard to believe I've only been here for two weeks. It seems like only a few days and a lifetime simultaneously.
Stewart Mottram, 11th August 2000

Thank you for the opportunity to fry our sausages.
The Hamiltons, 15th October 2000

....walked in over Table of Lorne by moonlight. Tricky – well hairy really – descent down cliff to bothy in dark, brilliant clear skies and views, temp <0°C.
Roger Boswell, 11th January 2001

Built a sweat lodge on the beach. Nothing like a good steam followed by a bracing sea breeze on the buttocks. Couldn't find any birches though. Many thanks for a great stay.
Sven, May 2001

Thank you for your hospitality – what a beautiful place. We anchored here last night and just popped ashore before continuing on to Tobermory. This shanty reminds us of the shanties at home – perfect. Home is the Falkland Islands and we are on our way to the Arctic Circle.
Alison and Andrez and baby Thomas, 5th May 2001

*Left in kayaks from Lochaline but got beaten at Ardtornish Point by force 5/6 winds and a spring tide pushing against us. Had 3 goes, but decided enough was enough, so took refuge for the night at Inninbeg. Came on here next day and have had a wonderful couple of nights, with a bit of kayaking and wood chopping during the day.
...*
Pete and Joe, 6th January 2002

*The common cormorant or shag [1]
Lays eggs inside a paper bag [2].
The reason, as you see, no doubt
Is that it keeps the lightning out [3].
But what these foolish [4] birds
Ignore is wandering herds
Of bears [5] will come with buns*

And steal the bags to keep the crumbs.

1. *The author has evidently confused Phalacrocorax carbo
    (Cormorant) with Phalacrocorax aristotelis (Shag, sometimes
    known as Green Cormorant). I have allowed the ornithological
    inexactitude in the interests of the sublimity of the verse. Ed.*
2. *The posterior abdomen of Phalacrocorax carbo, from which the
    egg emerges, is too big to fit inside the average paper bag. It
    seems more likely that the bird lays its egg on the ground, and
    then manoeuvres the egg into the bag with its bill, while holding
    the bag steady with its webbed feet. Bill and feet seem well
    adapted for this function. Ed.*
3. *The earliest recorded date of laying by Phalacrocorax carbo is
    5th April (Agnew, Ann Orth 1938;12:72). Thunderstorms are
    unusual before mid-May, but if the incubation period of 32 days
    is added to the date of laying of the final egg, lightning might
    indeed pose a threat to the clutch. It is possible that the paper
    bag also serves the function of keeping the eggs warm when the
    parent bird interrupts incubation to feed. Ed*
4. *The author here appears to be over-critical of the cognitive
    powers of Phalacrocorax carbo. There is no evidence that this
    species is less intelligent than other members of the genus, and
    a bird living at sea level can scarcely be expected to be
    conversant with the habits of a mountain-dwelling mammal! Ed.*
5. *Bun-eating has been described in the Himalayan Bushy-Browed
    Bear (Carstairs Ursine review 1924;iii:16), and may also occur
    in other species. It is perhaps remarkable that the bear's
    foraging range should extend to the coasts of Northern Europe.
    Like the squirrel, the Himalayan Bushy-Browed Bear has the
    habit of preserving surplus food for periods of famine, and
    paper bags no doubt serve as a convenient receptacle. Ed.*

Anon, April 2002

*I now know what happens in purgatory. They give you torrential
diarrhoea and make you go out every 30 minutes with your spade
into a wet and midgy night. I want to go to heaven, which has rows
of sparkling toilets.*

Chris Bacon, 10th June 2002